# Raise More Money
## from Your
# Business Community

## A Practical Guide to Tapping into Corporate Charitable Giving

**Linda Lysakowski, ACFRE**

# Raise More Money

## from Your
# Business Community

A Practical Guide to Tapping into
Corporate Charitable Giving

*Charity*Channel

# PRESS
™

Raise More Money from Your Business Community: A Practical Guide to Tapping into Corporate Charitable Giving

One of the In the Trenches™ series

Published by
CharityChannel Press, an imprint of CharityChannel LLC
30021 Tomas, Suite 300
Rancho Santa Margarita, CA 92688-2128 USA

http://charitychannel.com

ISBN: 978-0-9841580-8-9

Library of Congress Control Number: 2012930049

13 12 11 10 9 8 7 6 5 4 3 2 1

Printed in the United States of America

This and most CharityChannel Press books are available at special quantity discounts for bulk purchases for sales promotions, premiums, fundraising, or educational use. For information, contact CharityChannel Press, 30021 Tomas, Suite 300, Rancho Santa Margarita, CA 92688-2128 USA. +1 949-589-5938

# About the Author

**Linda Lysakowski, ACFRE**

Linda is one of fewer than one hundred professionals worldwide to hold the Advanced Certified Fund Raising Executive designation. With close to twenty years as a philanthropic consultant, she has helped dozens of nonprofit organizations achieve their development goals and has trained more than 20,000 professionals in Mexico, Canada, Egypt and most of the fifty United States, in all aspects of development.

Linda is a prolific writer. Her books include: *Recruiting and Training Fundraising Volunteers; The Development Plan; Fundraising as a Career: What, Are You Crazy?; and Capital Campaigns: Everything You NEED to Know.* Linda is also co-editor of *YOU and Your Nonprofit: Practical Advice and Tips from the CharityChannel Professional Community*; co-author *of The Essential Nonprofit Fundraising Handbook; and* contributing author to *The Fundraising Feasibility Study—It's Not About the Money.* She also published her first novel, *The Matriarch,* in 2011.

As a graduate of the Association of Fundraising Professionals (AFP) Faculty Training Academy, Linda is a Master Teacher and is a member of AFP's Professional Advancement Division. She serves on the board of the AFP Foundation for Philanthropy. She has received two AFP research grants.

Linda has been a frequent speaker at the international AFP conference and the CharityChannel Summit, and has spoken at numerous international, national and regional conferences.

 **Connect with Linda via CharityChannel**
http://charitychannel.com/cc/linda-lysakowski

# Acknowledgements

I would like to acknowledge all the companies and business leaders I have worked with throughout my careers in banking and in development.  Although there are too many to mention, there are a few who deserve special mention: Lawrence (Larry) Jilk and Jay Sidhu, both of whom in their tenure as bank CEOs showed the true spirit of corporate philanthropy. Tim Twardzik, Jon Scott and Kathy Kleppinger, who epitomize  corporate leaders who share their time to volunteer for the nonprofit community, talent in the form of excellent business skills, and treasure in the form of their financial contributions to the communities in which they live.  All of these and many more business leaders inspired me to write this book.

And, a special thanks to my many in-person and online colleagues who contributed to this book through their participation in surveys, social media postings, personal discussion, and chat groups.

I also want to thank Stephen Nill, my publisher, and Julie Thorp, manuscript editor, for their guidance and support in bringing this book to press.

# Contents

## Appendices

# Foreword

On one of those long, tedious cross-country flights, stuffed into an airplane seat and very much seeking diversion, I was serving due diligence to a rather large pile of professional fundraising magazines set aside for such a time as this. My mind was on the upcoming ACFRE certification process I was undertaking, and just how daunting it all seemed. In this tiny seat, 30,000 feet above all of my challenges, I happened upon an article Linda Lysakowski had co-authored on how to unravel the certification process.

Marveling at the precise outline of her piece, it was not lost on me that she had provided an email contact for anyone seeking additional support. Reflecting on my imminent path, I was assuredly seeking her additional support! After corresponding several times, many long phone calls and hours of indispensable professional advice it has become clear that this busy CEO is not just a philosopher in an ivory tower, she covets shared dialogue and hands-on work for the betterment of fundraising.

So it shouldn't come as a shock that Linda has written *Raise More Money from your Business Community: A Practical Guide to Tapping into Corporate Charitable Giving*, a personal, conversational, must-read book for any busy fundraising practitioner or head of corporate giving.

Finally, here exists a practical guide to demystifying a partnership that ultimately results in expansion of global community good. This book is a call to action for nonprofit and business leaders to recognize that in reality there is no faceless institution, but instead a huge opportunity through personal relationships fostered to help bring about lasting and sustainable changes in any community.

As fundraisers we've got to begin asking questions about the way we do business. What cornerstone forms the strategy or philosophy for the way we approach the priorities of our daily work? Is the old adage true for corporations, that they aren't giving because we aren't asking? And if we aren't looking for innovative ways to partner, someone, and I dare say it's those who are reading Linda's book, is getting the jump on us!

The precise span of this book covers compelling topics, which make it a valuable resource always to be tucked in a briefcase for quick reference at frequent opportune moments. It begins by asking us to take a new look at how we interpret current research regarding corporate philanthropy. Tactfully she touches on how the long-standing tradition of corporate foundation offices might actually be interfering with our efforts to build rapport within the local business community. These thought-provoking challenges are quickly followed by an abundant array of practical "getting started" steps initiated out of Linda's own extensive background in the profession and her personal business relations, including examples like MGM Resorts Foundation, Microsoft and Prudential Employee giving programs. Following the conclusion of how nonprofits and business can work more closely together, she has included robust appendices crammed full of valuable assets for every fundraiser's toolbox.

A significant challenge presents itself in writing a book that is perceptive, helpful and represents a palatable call to action. Thank you Linda for masterfully crafting such a useful tome as *Raise More Money from your Business Community: A Practical Guide to Tapping into Corporate Charitable Giving*. The unique culture of corporate giving in the United States should not and will not be lost as long as we are referencing your work.

Aristotle, ancient Greek philosopher is quoted to say, "First, have a definite, clear practical ideal; a goal, and objective. Second, have the necessary means to achieve your ends; wisdom, money, materials and methods. Third, adjust all your means to that end." With Linda's book, you now have that wisdom and method needed to make adjustments to your strategy and achieve your goals.

Joy C McKee, CFRE
Corporate Foundation Relations
Southern Adventist University

# Introduction

A number of years ago I was encouraged and inspired by a talk given by a bank president who received an award as outstanding volunteer fundraiser from his local chapter of the Association of Fundraising Professionals (AFP). In his talk he stressed the fact that as president of a regional bank, he was committed to giving at least 10 percent of the bank's profits to charity each year, and he challenged his colleagues in the business world to make a similar commitment. This community leader was a prime example of "putting your money where your mouth is." Not only was his bank very generous to the community but he himself had led numerous fundraising efforts for nonprofits in the community and he spent his vacations building houses for Habitat for Humanity. I have never forgotten his challenge and, after his talk, I became convinced that his challenge could be met if business leaders and nonprofits learned how, together, they could solve problems in their community, build stronger nonprofits and, at the same time, promote the business community as caring corporate citizens.

Although corporate giving traditionally has typically accounted for just about 5 percent of all philanthropy in the United States (in 2009 it shrank to just over 4 percent, but rebounded in 2010 to 5 percent), many organizations have counted on their local business community to provide funding, volunteers and in-kind products and services. In a struggling economy, many nonprofits are concerned that if this funding source dries up, their programs will suffer. Likewise many businesses and corporations are concerned about being able to continue their tradition of being good community citizens. Some forward-thinking business and philanthropic leaders have asked if that 5 percent figure could be increased if nonprofits and businesses learned more about corporate philanthropy.

In this book, I will briefly review the history of corporate philanthropy in the United States, talk about ways I believe that corporate philanthropy can be encouraged and increased, and reflect on its future.

It is my belief that some of the reasons corporate philanthropy remains a small segment of the overall giving in the United States are that the nonprofit community takes corporate giving for granted, does not understand the reasons businesses engage in philanthropic support, and does not approach the local business community using effective methods. I hope, through this book, to encourage nonprofits to consider new ways to approach their local business community, to truly engage business leaders in their organizations and to appreciate and recognize businesses for their contributions.

I am also convinced that nonprofits need to treat the business community in the same way they would treat a major individual donor. Research, cultivation and recognition are important not just with individual giving, but for business and corporate donors as well. We need to remember that businesses are run by people, employ people, and in most cases, sell their products and services to people. We need to get rid of the "Willie Sutton" philosophy which I will explain later in this book. We need to become more businesslike while, at the same time, retaining the spirit of the nonprofit sector. Through this book, I hope to teach nonprofits to better understand and learn how to work with their business community. My other goal is to help the reader encourage business leaders to become involved with their local nonprofit communities to help bring about lasting and sustainable changes in their communities.

## How This Book is Organized

**Chapter One: Corporate Philanthropy: Does It Actually Exist?** We start by exploring the types of businesses that operate in the United States and background information on the number of businesses and corporations in the United States and the types of structure for businesses. We will examine the concept of whether corporate philanthropy exists or not.

**Chapter Two: How Businesses and Corporations Give.** We will explore the various ways that corporations support their communities. We will discuss the role of small, medium and large corporations and businesses and the ways they currently support their communities and/or have supported them in the past. We will explore opportunities for nonprofits to gain support through gifts of cash, pledges to capital campaigns, event sponsorship, gifts-in-kind, and corporate volunteer programs.

**Chapter Three: What's Happening in the World of Corporate Philanthropy?** Here we will discuss the concerns corporate leaders have about the nonprofit sector. We will discuss recent trends in corporate giving and will elaborate on what types of funding corporations and businesses are increasing and which areas are decreasing. We will explore the reasons corporate leaders favor some types of support over other methods and how their policies have changed over the years. Based on feedback from corporate leaders, we will also discuss the ways corporations prefer being approached.

**Chapter Four: Why Corporations and Businesses Give.** This chapter will discuss what corporations and businesses are looking for in the nonprofits they support. We will talk about what businesses think nonprofits are doing right and what they are doing wrong. This chapter will offer insights into some common mistakes made by nonprofits when they approach the business community and how to avoid those mistakes.

**Chapter Five Getting Started: Identifying Business Prospects.** The first step in any giving program is finding prospective donors.

In this chapter we will talk about how to identify businesses in your company that are likely to support your organization. Both formal and anecdotal researching tools will be discussed. We will talk about some types of businesses you might approach in your community other than the "usual suspects."

**Chapter Six: Getting Started: Cultivation Tools.** Just as with individual donors, business leaders often need to be cultivated and made more aware of your organization before they're ready to be approached with the "ask." This chapter will explain the difference between cultivation activities and cultivation events and how you can use both to build relationships with your local business leaders.

**Chapter Seven: Getting Started: Making the Ask.** We'll discuss the practical steps you can use to start a corporate giving program or to increase results from your current efforts. In this chapter you will learn how to organize your approach in a more business-like manner. A step-by-step guideline to running a successful annual corporate and business appeal is included. We will discuss the annual business appeal, establishing a business advisory committee, recruiting business leaders to serve on your board and other ways to increase the results of your business and corporate fundraising.

**Chapter Eight: Assuring the Future of Corporate Philanthropy— the Nonprofit Role.** This chapter will discuss how the nonprofit community can use a more effective approach to the corporate sector. Suggestions will be presented for how the nonprofit can best present its case in order to secure corporate support.

**Chapter Nine: Assuring the Future of Corporate Philanthropy— the Corporate Role.** We'll conclude by looking at some of the novel solutions businesses can implement in order to continue to be good corporate citizens. Nonprofit leaders can share this advice and recommendations with business leaders wishing to start, continue or expand their corporate philanthropy programs. Trends in corporate giving are included in this chapter.

# Chapter One

## Corporate Philanthropy: Does It Actually Exist?

### IN THIS CHAPTER

···→ Corporate philanthropy or self-interest? Which of these explains why businesses might support your organization?

···→ What types of businesses are in your community?

···→ What do you need to know about these entities and how to approach them?

Is there such a thing as "corporate philanthropy?" Some would say no, that all giving by companies is self-motivated. In fact, when I posed this question on a discussion group, one answer which really caused me to stop and think was a reply from Rob Lavery, CFRE who said, "Simple, it ain't philanthropy." Others agreed, perhaps not so bluntly, that businesses looked for partnership opportunities as ways to promote their businesses, and that in-kind support and corporate volunteerism should not be viewed as philanthropy. Ann Rosenfeld, CFRE said that she feels one of the keys to obtaining support from the corporate community is

*Philanthropy*

Philanthropy—Literally, "love of humankind." According to one dictionary, "the spirit of active good will toward one's fellow persons, especially as shown in efforts to promote their welfare." Generally, the practice and philosophy of supporting, through financial and other contributions, programs, and campaigns conducted by charitable organizations.

demonstrating value for the company's employees. Many of my colleagues felt that all corporate giving had a self-serving impetus. So perhaps we need to look at the word, "philanthropy," to start this discussion. The literal definition of philanthropy is, "love of humankind," so those who argue that there is no true corporate philanthropy might be arguing that businesses and corporations do not care about human beings. Of course a corporation, a partnership or even a proprietorship, is a separate entity; it is not a human being. So, could they be right?

But wait, aren't all companies, even though they are separate entities, composed of human beings, whether they are owners, partners or stockholders? Do they care about humankind or profits alone?

No matter whose side of the following dilemma (see the sidebar "Two Diverse Opinions on Corporate Philanthropy") you are on, it is wise to heed the words of both. Milton Friedman makes a good point: businesses have a duty to make money for their stockholders and philanthropy is not their primary focus. However, Peter Drucker also makes a key point which, as nonprofit leaders, we must convey to our local business: Doing good is also good for business.

There are numerous companies that have built a reputation as outstanding corporate citizens, indicating that at least some of these subscribe closer to Drucker's theory than to Freidman's. The

## Two Diverse Opinions on Corporate Philanthropy

In 1970 Milton Friedman wrote that the only "social responsibility of business is to increase its profits…the corporation is an instrument of the stockholders who own it. If the corporation makes a contribution, it prevents the individual stockholder himself deciding how he should dispose of his funds." (Some might use this argument against workplace giving programs which will be discussed in a future chapter.)

In 1984 Peter Drucker offered another view, one that states that in order for a business to thrive, society must also prosper: "A healthy business, a healthy university, a healthy hospital cannot exist in a sick society. Management has a self interest in a healthy society, even though the cause of society's sickness is not of management's making."

Drucker's belief that a social contract exists between businesses and their communities gives us another viewpoint. In other words, contributions benefit both the community receiving contributions and the contributing company. Even Friedman admitted that the ability of an employer to improve the community from which the employer draws employees allows the employer to obtain more desirable employees.

Although Friedman and Drucker offer differing views of social responsibility and corporate philanthropy, both agree that there is reason for businesses to support their local communities. Friedman encourages corporations to support their communities by helping assure health care and life-support organizations. Drucker, on the other hand, places more of an emphasis on social responsibility, encouraging corporate management to act ethically and compassionately towards all of their stakeholders. While Friedman places his primary emphasis on the benefits of business to its shareholders, Drucker promotes the interest of the community at large.

**observation**

publication *Corporate Responsibility Magazine* lists the one hundred best corporate citizens annually (http://www.thecro.com). The current list can be found in Appendix B. One only needs to think about companies such as Ben and Jerry's, Starbucks, and Tom's Shoes to pose the theory that "yes, Virginia, there is such a thing as corporate philanthropy."

One of the most unique of these corporate philanthropists is Blake Mycoski, who actually did the reverse of what most venture philanthropists do. Most business leaders who have a philanthropic mindset seek to give away their money after they've been successful in business. Mycoski started from a very different perspective. He had the idea to be philanthropic first. On a trip to Venezuela he was moved by the need for shoes among thousands of barefoot children. These children were unable to attend school without shoes and suffered from many diseases brought on by being barefoot

A fairly recent trend in the giving world is known as "venture philanthropy." The term is borrowed from the concept of venture capital, since these donors think of themselves more as investors than as donors or contributors. Like venture capitalists, venture philanthropists are often willing to invest in a new program or a new organization, whereas more traditional donors, especially corporate foundations, tend to invest in the "tried and true."

Although venture capitalists often invest their money in a start-up businesses and remain a "silent partner," this is not the case with venture philanthropists. These people have generally made their money by being entrepreneurial in nature and they tend to invest in nonprofits that are on the cutting edge. However, they are far from being "silent partners." The usually want a voice in how the program is run, who is being served, or how the organization is managed. While it is great to have donors involved, you need to be careful that your organization's mission is not being compromised by the temptation of a high-dollar investment that might take you off your course, and result in "mission drift."

all of the time. He came home determined to do something about this problem and started Tom's Shoes with the idea of giving away a pair of shoes for every pair that he sold. Starting the business in his apartment and inviting three college interns to help him get the business off the ground, he was soon selling shoes and giving shoes away. As of 2009, Tom's Shoes has given away a million pair of shoes. This, of course, means that the company has *sold* a million pair of shoes. In this case the philanthropy came first and the successful business came as a result. Mycoski says, "Giving doesn't just feel good; it's good for business."

A question for business leaders:

*Did we really do good or did we just make ourselves feel good?*

**Blake Mycoski
President/CEOTom's Shoes**

The Green Mountain Coffee company, another example of a good corporate citizen released its first corporate responsibility report in 2006. In this report, the company CEO states, "We are focusing on measurement so we can understand the economic and social impact of the company and create indices so we can better focus those efforts." Michael Dupree, the company's vice president of corporate social responsibility, stated that "just the process of getting all that information in one place is valuable. It makes you think about and gain insight into what's working and what's not, so even if you never published anything, it's worthwhile." (A good lesson for nonprofits to heed, I would say.) We'll talk more in future chapters about measuring and reporting outcomes; but, this is one example of a business that is very aware of the importance of these measurements.

**Types of Business Entities**

Before you can understand, or defend, the world of corporate philanthropy, you need to understand the world of businesses and corporations. Knowing what types of entities exist and the differences between these types of entities will help you understand the different approaches that you can use with each that will be described in future chapters.

There are three major types of companies in the United States:

- ◆ Sole proprietorships

- ◆ Partnerships

- ◆ Corporations

As I write this book, there are approximately 16.4 million proprietorships (excluding farms), 1.6 million partnerships, and about 4.3 million corporations. Corporations, however, produce far more goods and services than the other two entities combined.

What are the differences between these types of entities? Sole proprietorships are typically owned and operated by one person or family, what we often refer to as "mom and pop" operations, although there are often large businesses that classify as proprietorships or that might have a limited number of stockholders, all of whom are family members. For example, I can cite a large department store chain, multi-billion dollar casinos, and other large companies that are, in one way or another, privately-owned, so you can't always judge a business's potential to give by its size or type of structure. The owners of a proprietorship are wholly responsible for all debts of the company, but also reap the benefits of all the profits.

A partnership is similar to a proprietorship except that there are two or more individuals who are responsible for the operation of the company. Many law firms and medical practices are partnerships, although in recent years, more of these types of businesses are operating as corporations, often a limited liability corporation (LLC). Partnerships may enjoy special benefits in tax policies. However, depending on the partnership structure and the jurisdiction in which it operates, owners of a partnership might have greater personal liability than they would as shareholders of a corporation.

Corporations are different from proprietorships and partnerships because no individual is responsible for the debts. If a company uses the designation, "Inc." it means it is incorporated and there are stockholders in the company. The corporation offers businesses the advantage of no personal liability for the company's debts. From the business standpoint, the disadvantage to any type of corporation, whether it is a C Corporation, an S Corporation, or an LLC, is that stockholders can vote out officers, even if they are the founders of the company. Keep in mind, though, that a corporation can have just one shareholder, in which case this is not going to be an issue.

While this is not meant to be legal treatise, nor should it be construed as legal advice, it is important to understand the differences in the types of businesses you are approaching for funding, who owns them, and what their motivations are. No matter what type of business structure the company has, its primary motivation is to make money, either for its owners or its stockholders.

**How Big is 'the Pot?'**

So, some questions you should strive to answer are:

◆ What is the pool of funds available from businesses and corporations in your community?

◆ How are other nonprofits attracting their share of these funds?

◆ How do the views of Friedman and Drucker fit with your views of corporate philanthropy or fundraising?

The economy of the United States is the largest national economy in the world. Its nominal Gross Domestic Product (GDP) was estimated to be $14.6 trillion in 2010. GDP is the market value of all final goods and services made within the borders of a country in a year.

Business profits during the 2010 were over $1.659 trillion, with after-tax profits at just over $1.25 trillion. Philanthropic giving from businesses and corporations in the United States totaled over $15.29 billion. Before you get too excited about the fact that businesses are giving away almost 10 percent of their profits, remember that this is not 10 percent of their *revenue*. And that still leaves much of their profits that are *not* being given to charities. I think we would agree that it is reasonable to expect that business owners, whether sole proprietors, partners or stockholders, receive a reasonable return on the investment of time, money and in some cases blood, sweat and tears. However, there is plenty of opportunity to divert some of this profit to help the communities in which these businesses operate.

Another way of looking at this is to compare corporate giving to individual giving on an "apples to apples" basis. While corporate giving in light of overall giving might seem insignificant, perhaps it is not as bleak as it appears as first blush.

Please note that the giving listed from corporations does not include marketing dollars that businesses often use to support sponsorships for nonprofit special events. Furthermore, some of the money given by corporate foundations is likely to be included in foundation giving.

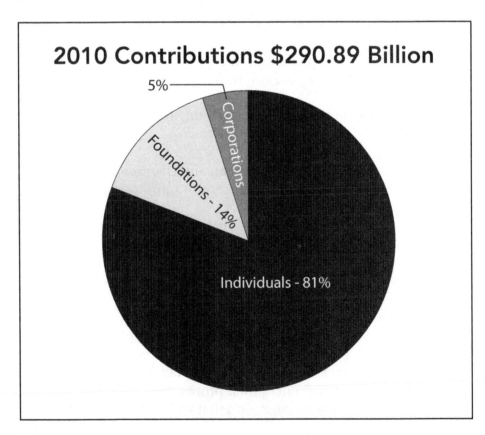

2010 Contributions $290.89 Billion

5%

Corporations

Foundations - 14%

Individuals - 81%

Another thing about these statistics that is sometimes deceiving is that the total pie consists of all philanthropic giving, including giving to religious institutions, which is generally given exclusively by individuals. If you take religious giving out of the picture, the pie chart looks somewhat different.

Please note: The pie chart on the following page assumes that all religious giving is from individuals, so the figures are not 100 percent accurate but give you some idea of how much is given by corporations to non-religiously affiliated nonprofits.

*How does corporate giving stack up against individual giving?*

Although some religious institutions promote tithing (giving 10 percent of one's income to charity) few individuals actually give at these levels. According to statistics, people earning less than $25,000 contribute an average of 4.2 percent of their household income to charitable groups, while those making $100,000 or more give an average of 2.7 percent of earnings. This

**Important Note to Statistics on Giving by Businesses and Corporations**

In a recent question posted on the CFRE International Network, development officers were asked whether they counted gifts by corporate foundations under foundation giving or corporate giving, responses were mixed as to how these gifts were counted. Some counted all gifts from corporate foundations under "foundation giving," other as corporate revenue and some even made the distinction based on how the gift was solicited. In light of these comments, I suspect that many corporate foundation gifts are being counted under foundation giving, thereby lowering the percentage of giving by corporations and exaggerating the amount of giving by foundations. As a frame of reference, there were 2,733 corporate foundations listed in the 2010 Report on Corporate Foundations from the Foundation Center.

practical tip

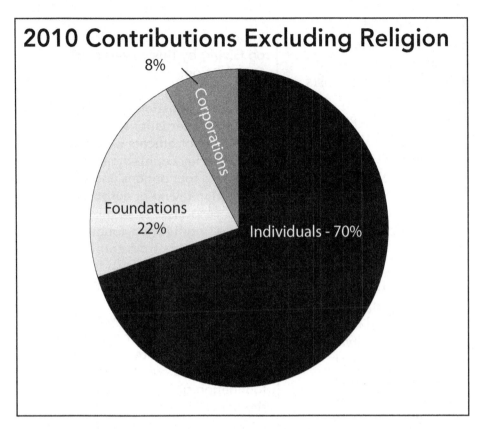

# 2010 Contributions Excluding Religion

8%

Corporations

Foundations
22%

Individuals - 70%

trend has been a consistent finding of Washington, D.C.-based Independent Sector, a nonprofit organization that has been tracking charitable giving since 1987.

Remember though, this is *income* (which might be compared to a business's *revenue)* we are talking about, not *disposable income,* which could be equated to a business's profits. So, in other words, if you earn $10,000 a month, have fixed expenses of $8,000 a month you have $2,000 of disposable income, and according to statistics, the average person earning $100,000 or more would be giving $270 of this disposable income to charity.

An example of how these statistics stack up for people with lower incomes would be a person who earns $2,000 per month, has $1,800 in fixed expenses and $200 of disposable income. According to statistics, the average person at this level of income would be giving $84 a month to charity.

I find it interesting that percentages of giving also vary in the corporate world. In fact, Fortune 100 companies give about 10 percent of their gross revenue, while, overall, companies contribute 13 percent of their gross revenue. Another interesting statistic is that Fortune 100 companies, in 2009, gave $559 per employee while overall, companies gave $650 per employee. So it seems that, as with individuals, companies with less income give a higher percentage of their revenue to charity. Remember these statistics when we get into identifying businesses in your community that you should be approaching.

|  | Individual Giving as percentage of income | Corporate/ business giving as percentage of revenues |  |
| --- | --- | --- | --- |
| Individual Giving from households with income of more than $100,000 | 2.7 percent | 10 percent | Fortune 100 companies |
| Individual Giving from households with income of less than $25,000 | 4.2 percent | 13 percent | All companies |

**Understanding Business Financial Terms**

It will help if you can understand how to read financial statements of businesses so you understand what its revenues are, not just its sales.

Business revenue is generally defined as income from activities that are ordinary for the business. In most businesses, revenue is from the sale of goods or services. However, banks and other financial institutions receive most of their revenue from fees and interest generated by lending.

Revenues from a business's primary activities are reported as sales. Most businesses also have revenue that is incidental to the business's primary activities. Your nonprofit might have income from things such as rental of property or services performed for other nonprofits or businesses, so this concept should be familiar to you. This is included in revenue but not included in net sales. It is clear that every business operates in order to earn profit. In virtually all cases the main goal of a business is making a profit. A business might have other goals but if it does not make a profit then the business will close its doors.

*What is business profit?*

The easiest way to explain profit is the income a company earned in a certain period of time. There are two types of profit, namely gross profit and net profit. Gross profit is not the actual profit of a business and it is found by deducting the cost of goods sold from net sales. Net profit is considered as the actual profit retained by a business and it is actually the difference between the revenue earned by the company and the expenses incurred.

If a company sold goods or provided services for a customer and received $2,000 cash and if the company paid $500 for the goods or services sold, the gross profit would be $1,500. If, however, salaries, rent and other expenses to do business in order to sell that product or service cost another $800 the *net profit* is $700.

*Example:*

| Goods sold | $2,000 |
|---|---|
| Less cost of goods sold | $500 |
| Gross Profit | $1,500 |
| Other expenses | $800 |
| Net profit | $700 |

It will be important for you to understand these concepts as you conduct research on potential business and corporate funders.

## To Recap

◆ Some people feel that there is no such thing as corporate philanthropy and that all giving by businesses is done on the basis of self-interest. Others believe that many businesses strive to be good corporate citizens and subscribe to the theory that they have an obligation and a benefit to building a strong community. There are many examples, however, of companies that pride themselves on being good corporate citizens and make philanthropic giving a high priority in their companies.

◆ Although the percentage of philanthropic dollars received in the United States from businesses and corporations is relatively small (just above 5 percent of overall giving in 2010), the dollars involved are not insignificant, amounting to over $15.29 billion in 2010. However, there are other ways corporations support their communities that might not be counted in these figures—gifts in kind, sponsorships, volunteerism, matching gifts and possibly even corporate foundation gifts that might not be counted in the total corporate gifts.

◆ Understanding the various types of business entities will be important in helping to develop strategies to approach these various companies for support. Your community will undoubtedly have numerous corporations as well as partnerships and sole proprietorships. Each of these has different owners and different philosophies on charitable giving and will need to be approached in different ways.

◆ The percentage of giving compared to overall income is actually higher in smaller companies than it is for Fortune 100 companies, just as the percentage of overall giving in individual households is greater for those who earn less than $100,000 a year than it is for household earning more than $100,000 a year.

◆ If you look at corporate giving compared to individual giving, the statistics show that both companies and individuals with less income actually give a greater percentage of their income to nonprofits. Businesses are actually more generous than individuals if you look at giving as a percentage of total revenue/income.

# Chapter Two

## How Businesses and Corporations Give

Although you might think that corporate support is minuscule compared to individual gifts, there are many benefits of building relationships with your business community. One thing to consider is the various ways businesses support their local communities. There are several ways businesses can support your nonprofit. These include:

◆ Gifts of cash

◆ Grants

◆ Event sponsorship

◆ Program sponsorship

◆ Multi-year commitments (pledges)

◆ Gifts-in-kind

◆ Support from corporate leadership

◆ Support from employees (workplace giving)

◆ Volunteer support

In a recent survey, I found that nonprofits received their support in all of these forms, with the greatest percentage of support coming from cash, gifts-in-kind and event sponsorship for those who completed the survey.

Let's talk about each of these types of support.

**Ways Businesses Give**

Businesses give in a number of different ways, so while one avenue might be closed to you with some companies, explore all the options. You might find another door open.

*Grants*

Some companies, particularly large corporations, have a corporate foundation. In this case, you will approach the foundation much as you would a private foundation, usually through a grant proposal. To determine if the company you want to approach has a foundation, you can use research tools such as http://www.grantstation. com or http://www.foundationcenter.com, or you can search the

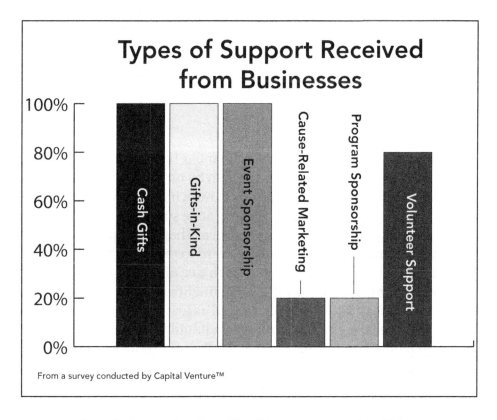

# Types of Support Received from Businesses

From a survey conducted by Capital Venture™

company's website or simply call it. However, you should know that just because the company has a corporate foundation does not mean that is the only way to approach that company. Banks, for example, might have a national or regional foundation; however, local branches could have discretionary money to disburse to local community organizations as well. Or a major corporation might have an employee foundation through which the employees make decisions about which local organizations they want to support. However, this same company could be approached through its corporate leadership, by those organizations that have been wise enough to develop relationships at the senior management level. Your organization could also receive gifts from the company's profits at the request of a senior level manager or corporate board member. So explore all your options.

One organization, for example, was successful in approaching a bank's foundation to fund one of its programs. The same organization secured an event sponsorship from the local branch of this bank, was the recipient of the bank's United Way employee giving program, and received an individual major gift from one of the bank's officers.

*Event sponsorship*

This is one area of corporate funding that has been decreasing in recent years. Many communities seem to be on 'event overload,' and the local business community simply cannot handle one more golf tournament, walkathon or gala dinner dance sponsorship. There are benefits to event sponsorship, however, that can appeal to some businesses. Some companies look forward to the opportunity to reward their employees by sending them to a dinner or to play in a golf tournament, or whatever the event might entail. However for other companies, these might be viewed as just one more burden on its staff—deciding which employees should fill a table at a dinner dance, juggling last minute changes, finding out spouse/partner names if they are attending with the employee. It might seem like as much work to them as it is to the nonprofit tracking all the attendees.

On the other hand, many businesses do like to have their company banner on display at an event that is being attended by their customers or prospective customers. Or, they might want their employees attending these events in order to 'mix and mingle,' thereby bringing in potential business for the company. The most successful event sponsorships will be the ones where the company sees it as a win-win situation for all parties.

Another advantage of event sponsorship is that it often is paid for from the company's marketing budget. If the company's philanthropic support dollars have been used up for the current year, it is often possible to tap into its marketing budget, which is usually more significant in size than its philanthropic budget.

*Program sponsorship*

Many companies prefer sponsoring programs and services rather than event sponsorships. Some good examples of this would be a company that pays for a scholarship each year to local colleges and universities. An accounting firm, for example, might want to sponsor a scholarship for finance or accounting majors. An architectural firm might sponsor a scholarship in that field, and so on. The business might even sponsor a chair in a department that relates to its business or prepares future employees of the company.

But you don't have to be a higher education institution to ask business to sponsor various parts of your program. If, for example, you are a local environmental group, a local business might sponsor a mile of the river you are cleaning up, or an acre of an organic community garden. Or, if yours is a human service agency, businesses could sponsor meals for a month for homeless youth in your community or a lecture on spotting drug addiction in teenagers. A business could sponsor a concert for a symphony or community chorus, a ballet performance, an exhibit at a museum or a zoo. Look at your programs and determine which of those might appeal to various companies.

*Multi-year commitments of cash*

One area of fundraising that usually yields a higher than average amount of gifts from corporate and business sources is the capital campaign. Often businesses will be happy to make a multi-year pledge for a capital campaign. One of the reasons for this is that capital campaigns generally offer named giving opportunities. If you're planning a campaign, do develop a strategy to ask companies to sponsor the ABC Company Learning Center, the XYZ Library, or the DEF Community Room. Another reason capital campaigns seem to generate a larger percentage of corporate giving is that because often local business leaders are involved in volunteering for the campaign and will solicit their own and other companies to make a contribution. (We will be talking more about how to use this concept to your advantage in your annual giving in a later chapter.)

Multi-year commitments, however, don't have to wait for a capital campaign. Many businesses would prefer to make a long-term commitment rather than be approached every year. For example, a business might want "first dibs" on the opening symphony performance each season, or want to assure that they sponsor an annual lecture series, or will want to help business students by making a ten-year commitment to funding a scholarship program. Some companies like to be able to budget these annual expenses so they don't need to be approached annually. However, I would caution against too many multi-year commitments because it can make it more challenging to go back to that company for an upgraded gift in years when they are doing well. Of course, on the other side of that coin is the fact that once your project is in the budget, most companies will honor that commitment unless the business suffers a severe setback.

*Gifts-in-kind*

Gifts-in-kind can be a mixed blessing for nonprofits. During tough economic times, many companies increased their gifts-in-kind while reducing their cash contributions. Many of your local businesses have unsold inventory and might be interested in contributing in-kind gifts because they cannot give cash donations at the same levels they did in the past. However, the old saying about not looking a gift horse in the mouth might not be true when it comes to gifts-in-kind. Don't just accept anything that comes along! You could find yourself being a property manager, caring for a horse, or trying to find a place to store a huge quantity of paint or furniture. I once found myself dragging boxes of books from the second-floor library of a donor. This is why having gift acceptance policies is so important!

Remember that the donor is required to assign a value to gifts-in-kind and that sometimes they inflate the value of these gifts in order to receive a more generous tax deduction. Gifts valued at more than $5,000 and that the IRS deems difficult to value must be appraised by an independent party, so you will need to discuss with the donor who will pay for this appraisal.

On the plus side, accepting gifts-in-kind can be extremely beneficial, especially when you are engaged in a capital campaign. Many of my clients have been able to significantly reduce the cost of their projects by having cement, paving, windows, carpeting, furniture, computer equipment, etc. donated by their local businesses. Some campaigns I've been involved with have had a division of volunteers solely involved in seeking gifts-in-kind for the project.

On the other hand, I've talked to nonprofits that have had 'dinosaur' computers donated that had to be trashed (and of course they had to pay to haul them away), gifts of artwork that did not fit the collection of a museum, and many other tragic stories that required a lot of time, work, and, sometimes, money, to resolve. You should always have a gift acceptance policy that includes how gifts-in-kind are treated. A sample gift acceptance policy is included in Appendix C. Although many of these policies will be useful in an individual

Some examples of how *not* having polices about gifts-in-kind can get your organization in trouble:

◆ One organization was offered a warehouse full of paint which they thought could help it with some facility renovations. It planned to sell the remaining paint, bringing in a nice profit. It turned out to be lead-based paint—not a bargain for anyone except the donor who wanted to empty his warehouse.

◆ A local stable offered a university a gift of a horse for its equine program. The university accepted the gift. Unfortunately, the university never started the equine program and had to house, care for and feed a horse for a number of years until it died. Maybe the university should not have heeded the proverb, "Don't look a gift horse in the mouth"!

◆ A local furniture company donated office furniture to a charity and highly over-estimated its value, causing havoc between the development office and the business office of the charity because the business office did not understand that the charity could not legally value the donated property.

**example**

major gifts program, you will find some that are relevant for business contributions, especially in regard to gifts-in-kind and named giving opportunities.

*Support from corporate leadership*

One of the areas that many people do not think about in relationship to their corporate giving program is the importance to building relationships with corporate leaders. There are several good reasons to do this:

◆ These leaders are often the sole decision maker for their company's philanthropic giving.

◆ These leaders can help you reach other corporate leaders and their companies.

◆ Contacts with these leaders asking for their company's support are often the entrée into their personal wealth and philanthropic giving.

In future chapters we will discuss how to build relationships with these corporate leaders. Do not forget about these advantages of corporate giving since these relationships might help you tap into some of that 85 percent of all philanthropic giving that comes from individuals.

*Support from employees (workplace giving)*

When you hear the words "workplace giving" you most likely think of United Way. United Ways have typically raised the majority of their money through workplace giving programs. Management is generally enlisted to support United Way at a leadership level and then encourage employees to support community agencies through payroll deduction into the United Way fund. If you are a United Way-supported agency, you will usually have the opportunity to make a presentation to local businesses about your agency. Don't pass up this valuable opportunity to tell your story.

In many communities, the local United Way might offer "designated giving" whereby employees can designate their United Way gift to go to a certain agency or agencies of their choice. Check with your local

---

**Workplace Giving Example: Bell Helicopter; Fort Worth, TX**

The Humanity Fund provides a convenient way to donate a portion of your income to hundreds of wonderful and deserving charitable organizations of your choice. Many of these organizations depend on the generosity of people like you to survive and fulfill their missions to enhance the lives of thousands of people across our community.

Employees can sign up to participate in the Humanity Fund, discontinue participation, or make changes to their contribution amount any time during the year. Changes to agency designation may be made once a year during the campaign.

◆ During the annual campaign an online form is available on the website and forms will be disseminated to all employees.

◆ At other times of the year, the form titled 'Humanity Fund' can be accessed on Outlook or through the Payroll department.

◆ Current level of enrollment will continue unless you change or cancel it.

The fund has its own board of employees. Employees can choose up to three charities to support each year. The Humanity Fund maintains a list of approved agencies, but employees may request that their favorite charity be added to the list of approved charities. Employees can contribute to both the Bell Humanity Fund and United Way.

stories from the real world

United Way to see if it offers designated giving. In a later chapter we will talk about how to develop a plan for workplace giving.

If you are not a United Way agency, you can check to see if there are any companies in your community that are not involved with United Way that might consider doing a workplace giving campaign for your organization. There are some companies that will allow other nonprofits besides United Way to talk to their employees and will set up a workplace giving program in their companies.

*Volunteer support*

In a recent study done by the Center on Philanthropy at Indiana University, Una Osili, director of research, found that many workplace giving programs are now encouraging employees not to just "write out a check," but to get personally involved by volunteering for the nonprofits as an even more meaningful way to support their community.

Brian A. Gallagher, president and CEO of United Way Worldwide agrees that getting employees more personally involved helps "donors and companies impact important social issues such as education, income, and health."

> *Companies are seeking deeper, year-round engagement with the nonprofits they serve. Corporate social responsibility goals are broader now, to incorporate not just employee giving, but also volunteering and other ways to be engaged with nonprofits in a community.*
>
> **Una Osili**
> **Center on Philanthropy**

Osili points out that nearly half of employees stop giving to nonprofits once they retire or leave their job. However, by engaging employees as volunteers, the nonprofits can create relationships with donors that transcend the workplace.

**Matching Gifts**

Many companies have matching gift programs,

whereby the company will match gifts made by its employees, including retirees in many cases. The Council for the Advancement and Support of Education (CASE) publishes an annual list of all major companies that have matching gift programs. These gifts often get credited (at least with soft credit) to the individual donor, but it is actually a gift from the company and needs to be credited that way. In some cases, the company will match 50 percent of an employee's gift, in other cases it is a 100 percent match or even higher. Most companies have a limit on gifts they will match on an annual basis, so in major gift appeals or capital campaigns in which you are seeking multi-year commitment, it will be important to structure the pledge payment carefully in order to take advantage of the employer's matching gift program.

Also, you will need to check each company's guidelines because some companies will only match gifts made to certain types of nonprofits. Usually education and health care are eligible for matching gifts; however most companies will not match gifts to religious institutions and certain other types of organizations.

## Examples of Matching Gift Policies

*LCG's Matching Gifts Policy*

*Policy:* LCG encourages community goodwill and charitable contributions, and may provide matching gifts to eligible employees towards personal charitable giving to accredited nonprofit 501(c)(3) organizations. This program is designed to give encouragement and assistance to these accredited and qualified institutions.

Procedures:

  A. Employee Eligibility

  1. LCG may match eligible charitable contributions for any salaried, regular employee with six continuous months of service towards any 501(c)(3) accredited organization.

  B. Eligible Gifts

1. The minimum personal contribution that will be matched in one calendar year is $25, and the maximum contribution that will be matched in one calendar year is $500;

2. Gifts must be LCG employee contributions made (not merely pledged), and must be in the form of credit card for on-line donations, check or money order;

3. Gifts must be made to organizations which are recognized as tax-exempt under Section 501(c)(3) of the Internal Revenue Code and are not "private foundations" as defined under Section 509 (a);

C. Ineligible Gifts

1. Non-cash gifts, real or personal property or volunteering your time and services;

2. Monetary gifts paid through a third party;

3. Dues or gifts to alumni groups that are not distributed to the higher education institution; or payments that cover the cost of services, tuition, books or student fees;

4. Gifts to booster clubs, religious organizations, individuals, sororities, or fraternities; personal businesses or ticket or merchandise purchases are not considered eligible contributions.

## Prudential and The Prudential Foundation

The Foundation will match gifts to eligible nonprofit organizations at a ratio of 1 to 1.

The minimum gift eligible for matching is $25 for contributions made by check, credit card, securities or life insurance.

The minimum gift eligible for matching made by payroll deduction is one dollar per pay period.

The maximum amount of gifts eligible to be matched by the foundation is $5,000 per individual, per calendar year, for all methods of giving combined.

Gifts must qualify as charitable contributions under the U.S. Internal Revenue Code. Gifts must be made from the individual's own funds not merely pledged, and must pass to the organization without reduction in value. *Only the tax-deductible portion of a contribution will be matched.*

*Eligible Participants:*

◆ Active full-time employees of Prudential Financial and participating subsidiaries

◆ Retired employees (direct giving only)

◆ Prudential part-time employees (twenty hours or more)

◆ Current and retired members of the Board of Directors

*Eligible Organizations:*

The philanthropic programs of The Prudential Foundation and of The Prudential Insurance Company of America and its subsidiaries support nonprofit, charitable organizations and programs whose mission and operations are broad and nondiscriminatory or whose activities address social needs or benefit under-served groups and communities. The right of religious organizations to maintain their identity is respected, but only their outreach efforts in the broader community are eligible to participate in the Foundation and Company programs. Most nonprofit organizations are eligible donees, provided they are located in the United States or one of its possessions. They must also be recognized by the Internal Revenue Service as tax-exempt and designated a public charity under Section 501(c)(3) of the IRS Code or as an instrumentality of a federal, state or local government as provided by Section 170(c)(1) of the Code.

*Ineligible Organizations:*

Any religious, political, veterans, fraternal or service organizations; alumni or athletic associations; honor societies; or professional associations are ineligible.

*What Types of Gifts Qualify?*

Personal check, money order, cashier's check or credit card payment gifts must be drawn against personal funds.

*Ineligible Gifts:*

◆ Contributions to scholarship funds where the scholarship recipient is designated by the donor; contributions in support of athletic programs, or athletic scholarships; payments in lieu of tuition, class dues, books or other student or alumni fees.

◆ Gifts made to or through third parties. This includes gifts made using family trusts, donor-advised funds at community foundations and any other contribution, which is not the direct gift of the donor's personal funds to the recipient organization.

◆ Gifts made, in whole or in part, with funds received from other people. This includes funds raised in walkathons and similar fundraising events. Only the donor's personal contribution can be matched.

◆ Gifts, which have not actually been made, for example, pledges. Once the gift has been completed, it is eligible for the program if it meets the guidelines.

◆ Other ineligible restricted funds include: dues for clubs; publication subscription fees; gifts to social, religious or political groups; gifts to honorary societies; bequests; church-related financial commitments; athletic programs; and other personal obligations.

◆ Private foundations are not eligible donees.

## An example of leveraging matching gifts programs

*Scenario A:* An individual wants to make a $50,000 three-year pledge to your campaign. The donor's company matches up to $10,000 a year. Therefore, the individual's gift now becomes $80,000.

*Scenario B:* This same individual is invited to make the commitment as a $50,000 five-year commitment, thereby bringing the total gift to $100,000.

## Scenario A

| Year | Employee's Gift | Company Match | Total Gift |
|------|-----------------|---------------|------------|
| Year 1 | $20,000 | $10,000 | $30,000 |
| Year 2 | $20,000 | $10,000 | $30,000 |
| Year 3 | $10,000 | $10,000 | $20,000 |
|  |  |  | $80,000 |

## Scenario B

| Year | Employee's Gift | Company Match | Total Gift |
|------|-----------------|---------------|------------|
| Year 1 | $10,000 | $10,000 | $20,000 |
| Year 2 | $10,000 | $10,000 | $20,000 |
| Year 3 | $10,000 | $10,000 | $20,000 |
| Year 4 | $10,000 | $10,000 | $20,000 |
| Year 5 | $10,000 | $10,000 | $20,000 |
|  |  |  | $100,000 |

Is it worth it to extend the pledge period? If you don't need the funds within three years, most definitely, yes!

**example**

### Gifts of Cash

Obviously, we all want cash! And judging from the statistics we discussed in chapter one, there is lots of it to go around. So how do you determine how much cash your local business community has and how much it is willing to give?

Well, one way is to ask! "Who do I ask?" you wonder. There are several answers to this question:

- ◆ Do some preliminary research.

- ◆ Ask those who *might have* the answers (colleagues, other nonprofits, local business leaders).

- ◆ Ask those who *for sure have* the answers (the business owners and executives in your community).

*Research*

One way to research companies is to obtain a copy of the company's annual report. If it is a publicly held company it will publish an annual report to stockholders.

Another important thing to note is that a spouse's employer might have a matching gift program. For example, Ms. Donor, a board member, usually makes her gift in her name alone. If Mr. Donor's company has a matching gift program, Ms. Donor might be persuaded to make her gift in the name of Mr. and Ms. Donor in order to take advantage of the matching gift program her spouse's company offers. This could also include staff of your nonprofit, which itself would not match gifts from your employees; however, staff members might have spouses that work for matching gift companies.

practical tip

If the business is a privately held company, this kind of research might be a little harder to track down but you can subscribe to services that can do corporate research. You might want to check out some of the resources below.

Check the company's website; often information about the company's giving policies and its annual report can be found on the website.

For corporate foundations, you can usually find their information on the Foundation Center directory or you can research the 990 forms on http://www.guidestar.org.

Your local chamber of commerce and local *Business Journal* are often good sources of information.

If the company is publicly held, it is required to file a proxy statement. This statement will give you some valuable information, such as a list of board members, their ages and occupations and a list of other boards on which they serve. (Remember these are for-profit boards which operate differently from your nonprofit board, and officers are generally compensated for their service on for-profit boards.) Another section

> ### Definition: Proxy Statement
>
> A document which the SEC requires a company to send to its shareholders that provides material facts concerning matters on which the shareholders will vote.

of the proxy statement will provide information that includes a list of top-ranking corporate executives and lists their annual compensation as well as other benefits they receive. This information will be valuable in building relationship with the corporate leaders who could be potential individual donors to your organization.

Check the company's website. It might contain information about the forms of giving this company tends to use and the specifics of what types or organizations the company supports. For example, a visit to the website of a large financial institution such as http://www.wellsfargo.com will tell you the types of organizations they support, the kinds of giving and the types of organizations they do not support, and will give you a link to an application form. Checking the website of a privately held company might be a bit trickier. One of the largest independently-owned department store chains in the United States, for example, http://www.boscovs.com, under "Boscov's in the Community," at first glance shows mostly cause-related marketing efforts that support local nonprofits in the communities where stores are located. However, if you search the "News Releases" section, you will find evidence of significant contributions from the company and its owners.

Ben and Jerry's Ice Cream, known for its social responsibility, has a link to its foundation on the http://www.benandjerrys.com website. The foundation lists numerous funds, some focusing on Vermont-based agencies (its home office location) and others nationally-based. Links on the foundation's web site will show you exactly which organizations the foundation supported over the past three years, the amount of the grants given, and the purposes of the grants. A little effort and a lot of time on your part will help you narrow your search and learn more about the companies you want to approach.

Follow your local newspapers, particularly your local business journal, which usually publish lists such as top employers in your community, top executive salaries, and top sales revenue, etc. These publications often publish a "Book of Lists," which is a handy resource to track key statistics on local businesses, such as number of employees, top-paid executives, revenues, etc.

Check the donor lists of other nonprofits. One word of caution, however, is that just because a company supported other nonprofits

---

Some resources to help research companies include:

> http://www.hoovers.com

> http://www.foundationcenter.com

> http://www.grantstation.com

 practical tip

in your community does not necessarily mean it will support *your* organization. Some sources you can check to see who is supporting other nonprofits include:

◆ Annual reports

◆ Websites

◆ Newsletters

◆ Donor walls within the facility

◆ Attending other nonprofit events that are sponsored by local businesses.

You might want to contact members of AFP if you are a member of your local chapter and ask with which businesses they've been successful. This preliminary research will give you an idea of the size of gifts your local businesses might consider. But, remember, you need to make the case for support for *your* organization. You will also need to build relationships with the decision makers of these companies and/or involve their employees in your organization.

*Ask those who might know*

There is an amazing amount of public knowledge out there about both businesses and individuals. Those who might be privy to some of that knowledge about your local business community include your board members, your staff, your volunteers (especially the development committee) and community leaders (especially business leaders such as bankers, corporate CEOs, accountants and financial planners). While you do not want to ask anyone to divulge confidential information, there are ways to find out which businesses in your community are doing well and which ones are not. One of these methods is conducting a series of screening meetings aimed at refining the research you've already done on your call business community.

At first glance, you might think that your organization does not have the "movers and shakers" or business leaders on your board who could help identify business prospects. Before writing off your board members, consider doing some brainstorming on prospective business donors and volunteers. You might be surprised at the connections your board has in this regard.

**Lessons Learned**

Here are some real-life stories that helped me learn not to "judge a book by its cover."

*Scenario # 1*

> A small community library was in the beginning stages of a capital campaign. I was on my way to a screening and rating session to identify prospects with whom the board members might have contacts they could solicit for donations to the campaign. One of the prospects who lived in the service area of the library was the senior partner in one of the state's largest law firms. I knew this prospect could be the single largest donor to the campaign if we could find a board member that might have a contact with this business leader. I mentally went through the list of board members in my head and was convinced that there was only one board member who *might* move in the same circles as the prospective donors.

> To my surprise when I got to the meeting and began the process of reviewing names, the board chair, a factory worker, spoke up and said, "I can talk to him. He is my cousin." Don't judge a book by its cover, indeed!

*Scenario # 2*

> A human service agency had a small and ineffective board— none of its members could read a financial statement, none had an understanding of marketing or fundraising, and most didn't understand the organization's complex funding structure which was heavily based on government funding.

As the board began to transform itself into a more sophisticated and knowledgeable board, one that could actively engage in community development and fundraising, one of the board members spoke up and said she felt it might be time for her step down. She had never participated at board meetings, probably because she really did not understand her role as a member of the board. However, she had a recommendation for someone to take her place. I confess. I trembled at the thought that her replacement would be another ineffective board member. It turned out her recommendation was her stock broker—the vice president of the county's largest brokerage firm. Her broker make an excellent board member, giving generously and inviting others to participate. As an added bonus, the original board member, pleased that we had accepted her suggestion, gave a planned gift to the organization at the advice of her broker— the largest gift this organization had ever received. It was a gift that could have been lost if we had judged a book by its cover.

There is a "brainstorming form" in Appendix I that can help you first determine the links your board and staff have with businesses in your community.

## Screening Sessions

After this initial brainstorming, you will need to do more qualifying research to determine the best linkages, the ability of the company to give, and its interests. This usually is best done in the form of screening and rating sessions. It is generally easier to get information from screeners on businesses than it is on individuals. A side benefit of using this approach to identify prospective business donors is that this could be a good first step in preparing your organization to screen individual donors for a major gift program!

There are basically three ways in which to conduct screening for corporate prospects. This method also works well for individual major donor prospects. Select your committee members very carefully and make them aware that the information shared in these meetings is *very confidential.* If your board or committee volunteers have never done screening before, explain to them that this method is used routinely in most organizations and is the best way to determine the key ingredients of a major gift, whether it is from an individual or from a company—Linkage, Ability and Interest (the LAI Principle). If you are working with a consultant, this person will generally lead the screening meetings. If you do not have a consultant, be sure that the meeting is led by an experienced group facilitator. It will be very important to keep the group on task and explain the methodology and reasons behind the screening meeting to those who are not familiar with the process.

---

**The LAI Principle**

**Linkage:** Who has the best connection with this prospective donor?

**Ability:** How much could this prospective donor give?

**Interest:** Is the prospective donor interested in your organization and its programs?

Without all three of these components, it is impossible to get a major gift from an individual, a foundation or a business.

**principle**

---

It is also crucial to start with a preliminary list. It is hard to get a brainstorming or screening session started with a blank slate. Prepare a list of corporate donors and/or sponsors to your organization, vendors or other businesses that you feel might have the potential and the interest or connection to your organization. This can be developed from your initial brainstorming session, using the sample form included in Appendix I. You should look particularly at businesses that have a natural connection to your organization. For example, if there is a manufacturer of crayons or toys in your community and your organization is one that deals with children, there is a natural fit. If yours is an organization that primarily serves the elderly, a chain of pharmacies might have an interest in supporting your organization. List the giving history of these businesses, if they are already donors of any type of gifts including sponsorships and gifts-in-kind. Some preliminary research will help determine the level of support these companies have provided for other nonprofits in your area. Remember that your goal is to raise the sights of businesses that might be supporting you in a minimal way to think about more significant forms of support. List their largest gift and most recent gift. Provide a column for each of the key ingredients—Linkages, Ability and Interest. Be sure to mark the sheets "*Highly Confidential.*"

Now to the three screening methods:

1. *The Open Screening Session*—Invite the group to assemble in a quiet room and open the discussion with brief explanation of the process, its importance to your organization and why they were selected to help with this task. Then distribute the lists and discuss each company on the list, attempting to determine the best *linkage*—who knows the decision makers of this company best or would be the best person to make the "ask." Often there will be several linkages and the task of this group is to determine the best solicitation team. For example, suppose

---

For all three methods the screening committee could include:

❑ Board members

❑ Staff

❑ Development committee members

❑ Members of a corporate appeal committee

❑ Organization volunteers with broad community connections in the business world

practical tip

you have a local prominent insurance agent on your prospect list. Perhaps one board member says, "Oh, she is my insurance agent; I can contact her." But perhaps another volunteer is a business owner and uses this same insurance agent for all her company, home and boat insurance. This volunteer might have a much stronger connection with the insurance agent. Or perhaps the best plan is for both the board member and the volunteer to call on this prospect together. Next, try to determine ability—what *could* this company give to your organization if so motivated? Without revealing confidential information, the screening committee members often can guesstimate the company's net worth and/ or sales figures using public information. Then try to determine *interest*—does this company have knowledge of your organization? Is this a cause

> ### Determining interest is crucial to success
>
> Once when interviewing prospective donors for a youth-serving organization, I asked a casino executive about contributing to this worthy organization. The answer was that the casino might consider a small gift, but most of the company's funding went to support health care and organizations that focused on providing programs for senior citizens. Makes sense. Who are the casino's biggest customer? Seniors!
>
>  stories from the real world

they are known to support? Is there a specific program of your organization or part of your project that you think would interest them? Screening committee members might have knowledge of this prospect's areas of interest from other boards on which they serve or other relationships they might have with the prospect. As each company is discussed, complete the form with the *linkages, ability* and *interest* named. The advantage of this method is that there is discussion and consensus; the disadvantage is that some people feel uncomfortable discussing prospects. Most people, however, feel more comfortable discussing business prospects than they do individual donor prospects because it is far less personal. In fact, you might find this a good introduction to the process that can be helpful later when you use this method to identify *individual* donors. Some information is likely to emerge about business leaders that will help your individual major gifts program.

2. *The Closed Session*—This method is very similar to the first, except that instead of discussing each company among the group, participants in the session are asked to complete the answers to the *linkage, ability* and *interest* sections to the best of their own knowledge. Each person works independently without discussion among the group. Lists are then collected and the person in charge reviews the lists and determines the consensus of opinion. The advantage of this method is that people might feel freer to comment on prospects if they are doing it confidentially; the disadvantage is that once the lists are collected (screeners should mark their name on their list before turning it in) there is a lot of guesswork and perhaps follow-up to clarify what a screener has written. Without the open discussion it is sometimes difficult to figure out why one person thought this company had the ability to give $100,000 and another suggested $1,000.

3. *The Private Screening Session*—This method is similar to the first except that it is held one on one with a staff member and a screening committee member. The list is reviewed with screening committee members one at a time in the privacy of the person's office or other location. The advantage of this method are that it is easier to schedule people at their convenience than getting them all together in one room. The open discussion takes place between the staff and the screening committee member. The disadvantage is that it takes a lot more staff time to meet with screening committee members individually. The lack of open discussion might mean follow up to clarify major differences of opinion.

In all three methods, you will want to make sure to encourage screeners to add their own names to the list. Seeing the list will often jog people to think of other potential corporate and business donors for your organization. Whichever method you use, you will most likely uncover some hidden 'stars' among your current business connections and uncover new prospects along the way.

*Ask those who for sure know*

Research and screening can help qualify your corporate prospects to a great extent but, of course, there is nothing like "getting it straight from the horse's mouth." Ask the company! (Or, more accurately, its decision makers.)

In a future chapter we will deal more with building relationships with your local business community, but it all comes down to the old adage that says "ask for money and you will get advice, ask for advice and you will get money." This is especially true when it comes to raising money from your business community. You should meet with your local business leaders on a regular basis, involve them on your board and committees, schedule advice-giving meetings with them, and invite them to cultivation events. (More about all of this in future chapters.)

Once you've established a relationship with business leaders, ask how their business is doing. If they are doing well, they will be happy to share their success stories with you. If they are not doing so well, you will save yourself and the business leader the embarrassment of asking for gift that is beyond the company's capability. Remember that the answers to this question might be relative. "Boy we've had a terrible year this year," might mean that instead of a billion dollars in profits, they only made several hundred millions! During this process you can also ask them about the ways they

> Ask for money and you'll get advice; ask for advice, and you'll get money.

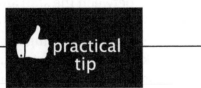
practical
tip

might consider supporting your organization. If cash is not one of those ways, you can then explore some of the other options.

Remember to do your initial research on the company's website and other electronic researching tools. Refine this research by asking volunteers for input and finally ask the company's leadership itself. Just as most program officers at a foundation are happy to answer questions about the foundation's interests, most business leaders will appreciate the fact that you took the time to talk to them first and didn't waste their time reviewing inappropriate requests.

Don't forget that business leaders are also often top prospects for major individual gifts. Once you establish a relationship with the leaders of businesses, you can often get them more involved in your organization and serving as board members or volunteers. You can eventually cultivate them for a major gift from their personal wealth.

> *Please don't waste my time—know my business and its charitable giving guidelines and come prepared.*
>
> **Christina Gold**
> **CEO, Western Union**

Of course, the fact that you have business leaders involved in your organization is a great way to involve other business leaders, obtain gifts from those businesses, and cultivate additional individual gifts from other business leaders.

The volunteer time itself can be very valuable to your organization. One organization was successful in saving the cost of a full-time salaried position by having an enthusiastic company owner provide a loaned executive to the organization.

Illustrating how valuable volunteer time can be is an example from a mentoring agency. One of the organization's board members, who had served as a mentor himself, was so impressed with the organization and its programs that he decided to loan the organization one of his key executives for a year. The board member paid the salary of this executive for a full year while he worked

**Keeping up with current guidelines is critical**

One environmental organization had been the recipient of a bank's generosity in the past, so when it was preparing a prospect list for a new appeal it was about to launch, this bank rose to the top of its prospect list. However, when representatives approached the bank, they did not do their research on its funding priorities. It seems the bank, which had in the past been supportive of environmental groups, now focused its giving in three areas: health, hunger and homelessness. Needless to say the organization did not get a gift from the bank. Lesson learned: Do your homework!

practical tip

as an executive of the nonprofit. This windfall came at exactly the right time for the agency, just as a large federal grant was about to end and the agency needed to ramp up its fundraising efforts. They now had a full-time executive with lots of business contacts, and an amazing amount of enthusiasm for the agency. This loaned executive said it was a great experience for him as well and is certain that this experience will make him an even more valuable employee when he goes back this regular job. Of course, he could just decide to remain in the nonprofit world. He will be a valuable asset to his community either way.

**To Recap**

◆ There are many ways you can have your local business community support your nonprofit's work. Outright gifts of cash; multi-year pledges, gifts-in-kind, gifts from corporate leaders, corporate foundations and employees are some ways to gain corporate support.

◆ Don't forget about volunteers. Corporate leaders can serve in high level positions including board membership, executive coaches, technology consultant, providing accounting or legal services, serving on advisory committees, development councils, and campaign cabinets.

◆ You should try to determine how much is likely to be given by your local business community. Brainstorming with board members and community volunteers to identify companies that might support your organization can help add to your internal research of the local business community. Invite a small team of volunteers to help you review potential business donors and determine who has the best linkage with these prospective donors.

### Remember That It's All Relative

One consultant was conducting a planning study interview for a proposed capital campaign. One key business leader was enthused about the cause, but told the interviewer he wasn't sure how much he could give because "business was bad." He mentioned that he had to close some of his offices. As the interview progressed, however, he just happened to mention that he would make his decision about the level of his commitment to this organization after he finished paying off the $50 million pledge he recently made to his university.

practical tip

# Chapter Three

## What's Happening in the World of Corporate Philanthropy?

### IN THIS CHAPTER

- ⋯➔ What trends in the corporate world affect charitable giving?

- ⋯➔ Do corporate leaders use a bad economy as an excuse not to give?

- ⋯➔ What changes have there been in the ways companies give?

The world of business is changing. Corporations, like nonprofits, are trying to do more with less. For many companies this means they have fewer employees trying to pump out the same amount of work they did in years when belts were much looser. So, there might not be as many top-level and mid-level managers available to serve on boards and volunteer committees. It's hard to commit to meetings and fundraising activities when you're already putting in fifty or sixty hours a week at work (and probably getting paid for forty!). This is one of the leading reasons why nonprofits are finding it harder and harder to involve business leaders in volunteering for their organization. However, many businesses, especially those in the service industry, recognize the need to set an example for employees by allowing management to remain involved in community activities.

*Where can you find business leaders to volunteer for your nonprofit?*

You will probably find some key management people involved in service clubs and other activities. This is a good place to start looking for company executives and middle management who do still take the time to get involved in their communities.

Some Service clubs include:

◆ Civitan

◆ Jaycees

◆ Kiwanis

◆ Lions Clubs International

◆ Optimists

◆ Rotary International

◆ Sertoma

◆ Soroptomists

*Taking Care of Business*

Business is moving at lightning speed. Everyone expects employees, outside contractors, vendors and customers to make instant decisions and to provide an almost-instant turn-around time. The world of technology has improved the way we do business, but it also results in sometimes unreasonable expectations. Gone are the days when someone would say, "Mail me a proposal and we'll get back to you in a few weeks." Now it is more likely to be, "E-mail that proposal this afternoon and we'll get back to you in a few weeks." The person wanting information wants it instantly. However, sometimes acting on that information takes just as long, if not longer, than it did in the past. Decisions might not be as forthcoming as the expected information is, simply because there is so much communication going on within any company that it is hard to get to the decision makers. Nonprofits are not exempt from this expectation to deliver information on a timely basis, but should also be prepared to deal with the frustrations of waiting for a decision. If you can't make your case to the business leader in ten minutes, you might not have a chance to come back when you're better prepared. If the business does need time to discuss your proposal, be sure to ask when a decision will be made and follow up right after the anticipated decision date.

## Two sides of competition

*Are you competing with your prospective funders?*

Sometimes businesses might also see the nonprofit as a competitor. Living in the entertainment capital of the world, one of the common themes I hear from the arts community is that the local gaming industry is not supportive of the arts because the arts groups are seen as competition. After all, casinos are holding performances every night of the week themselves, so why would they encourage people to go see the ballet, a concert or an art exhibit when they could come to the casino and tour an art museum, see a live concert or a dance performance. To bring it closer to home, think about whether or not your local florists and gift shop owners might want to support your hospital or museum if you have a gift shop that sells flowers and gift items that they sell in their stores. While many nonprofits can successfully operate a for-profit arm of their agency, you need to be aware not only of Unrelated Business Income Tax laws (UBIT) but also of how your operations might be perceived as competition by your local business community.

*Can you help your funders set themselves apart from their competition?*

Competition is keen within the for-profit sector; if you don't think this is true, drive around your block and count the number of banks you see. Businesses are looking for ways to set themselves apart from the competition. They try to gain the competitive edge, to convince you that their product or service is better than the other bank, or store, or insurance company down the street. If you can develop a win-win strategy, you will be ahead of the game.

For example, one organization that was located near a popular locally-owned restaurant took advantage of a competitive situation for this restaurant. A new chain restaurant opened nearby and was taking a lot of the original restaurant's business. The nonprofit approached the locally-owned restaurant and suggested a partnership. The organization would invite its supporters to a special night out at the restaurant. In exchange for this, the restaurant agreed to donate a percentage of its revenues on that night to the nonprofit. This helped both partners and the restaurant felt that the organization was really trying to help it out.

Does all this talk about competition sound familiar? In other words, businesses have many of the same problems you have in your nonprofit. You can most likely empathize with the local business owner who might be trying to make a case for why her business deserves support, maintain excellent service even though he's had to let staff go, and stay on top of all the latest trends in her field. These are the same issues you are dealing with every day. So who has time to try to keep on top of business trends, too?

You do!

You must!

The more you get to know your business community, the better you will understand the concerns and needs of the business community, and the better you will know how to approach business leaders for support. If you're not sure what business groups are in your community, try contacting your local chamber of commerce and find out when and where they meet. Remember that in many communities there is more than one chamber of commerce. You might have several chambers serving different geographical locations. In my community, for example, there are at least four

Here are some questions to ask yourself about how well you're keeping up with trends in your community and globally in the business world:

❑ Does our organization belong to our local chamber(s) of commerce or economic development association?

❑ Does our staff attend meetings and participate in activities of these groups?

❑ Do we subscribe to the *Wall Street Journal* and local business journals?

❑ Do we regularly make presentations at meetings of groups such as Rotary, Lions Club, Kiwanis, and other groups where business leaders are likely to be found?

❑ Do we regularly meet with business leaders to find out what is happening in our community?

❑ Do we talk to our vendors about their businesses?

❑ Do we have representatives of our local business community serving on our board?

❑ Do we ask our board members and members of our development committee to give us insight into their companies and the business world in general?

❑ Do we involve members of our local business community on various committees and as program or fundraising volunteers?

practical
tip

geographically-based chambers: a women's chamber, an Hispanic chamber, an Asian chamber and an African-American chamber, in addition to an economic development association. Some communities also have a manufacturers' association. All of these should be on your list. This is a good place to get started. You can also ask board members, staff members, donors and volunteers about the business groups to which they belong. In a later chapter, we will talk more about joining and getting involved in local business groups.

**Businesses Have Many of the Same Concerns Nonprofits Have**

What are some of the concerns your local business community might have that could affect your charitable requests?

For some companies, it might be a matter of survival. If the company has been forced out of business due to a poor economy or other circumstances, obviously you will not be receiving any further contributions from this company. On the positive side, the staff members being laid off will now be looking for jobs and there could be a possibility that these employees will be seeking jobs in the nonprofit sector or have time to volunteer for your nonprofit organization. This could be a great opportunity for your organization to pick up a staff person or volunteer with extensive business experience.

Mergers are another big fact of life in today's business world. One of the devastating results of mergers and acquisitions is that nonprofits who have been receiving contributions from two or three banks, for example, now have one bank from which to request funding. Again, mergers could result in staff layoffs that might actually benefit the nonprofit community. There is also the opportunity to invite the surviving, stronger company to consider supporting your organization in a bigger way. This might not always be successful but it's worth a try.

Another trend is for companies to relocate to an area of the country that has a lower cost of living and/or a better taxing structure in order to show a greater profit, or to leave this country altogether. Although this can be disastrous for nonprofits depending on this company's support, there could be new companies moving into your area that could be potential supporters. You should make plans to meet with these company leaders as soon as possible after they relocate to your area. Becoming involved with your local chamber of commerce is a good way to find out what companies are moving into your area.

Keeping your finger on the pulse of your local business community is critical to knowing who is moving in, who is moving out, who is being bought, who is buying out another company, and who among their staff is in the job market because of these changes.

**Economic Factors**

Is a poor economy just a handy excuse for the local business community to stop (or not start) supporting the nonprofits in the community?

Call me the eternal optimist, but I don't think it is! I've worked

One organization was devastated when one of its community's major banking institutions was bought out by a larger bank whose headquarters was in an adjoining county. The local community assumed that since the bank was no longer headquartered in its community, the support it had received in the past from this bank would be gone. However, it took a negative and turned it into a positive: The CEO of this new bank had made a statement that, while not intending to do so, was misinterpreted by the local community. His statement sounded, to many in this smaller community, as though members of their community were "country bumpkins" compared to the larger city that served as headquarters of the acquiring bank. The CEO, in an effort to show his support for this new community in which his bank was attempting to make inroads, facilitated an extremely generous gift from the bank to a nonprofit's capital campaign when he was approached by one of the leaders of the bank his bank had acquired. The publicity received for this donation made the community forget that it had been slighted earlier by this CEO.

stories from
the real world

with a lot of business owners and corporate leaders in my career, and I am convinced that most of them *do* care about their communities. Many of them are truly committed to philanthropy. We can hardly doubt that these shining heroes exist when we hear about Bill Gates, Warren Buffet and the other billionaires who have accepted the challenge to give away most of their money to charity. This is not an entirely new phenomenon. Many wealthy industrialists such as Andrew Carnegie, who was called a "robber baron" in his time, subscribed to the gospel of wealth that dictates that those who have great wealth should give it away during their lifetime in order to enjoy the fruits of their generosity by seeing firsthand the good that their contributions accomplish. While you might not have Gates or Buffet living in your own backyard, every community has successful businesses and business leaders who are people of great wealth.

Of course, this great wealth is actually in the form of personal wealth that has been accumulated by individuals because of their great business acumen. In other words, they make great profits in their business in order to accumulate great wealth for themselves. So, should we focus our energies on asking the businesses to contribute or should we use our business connections to build relationships with the business owners? I say we should do both. The two are not mutually exclusive. In fact, focusing on both can be a great approach to raising your overall fundraising income. This is one reason the corporate/foundation office of a nonprofit is often not successful. It fails to engage staff members who are adept at building relationships with corporate leaders, but focuses, instead, on staff members who are good researchers and proposal writers.

### The Bottom Line

Most business leaders are concerned about the bottom line, which means more profit for the owners or stockholders, better salaries and working conditions for their employees, and more taxes being paid to the communities in which they are located. But within the profit margin, there are still opportunities for businesses to be philanthropic, to invest in their communities and to seek marketing opportunities for the business. In a poor economy, there will be less profit for the owner/stockholders, lower salaries and fewer jobs for employees, but perhaps more of a need to market the business. So during a poor economy, you might want to focus your efforts on things such as corporate sponsorships, gifts-in-kind and cause-related marketing. (We will discuss these more in future chapters.) Don't forget, also, that even in a poor economy there are some businesses that not only survive, but thrive. I've often suggested to nonprofits that bankruptcy attorneys could be a prime target for philanthropic giving during a tough economic time, because many of them are making money! Many entrepreneurs are very creative at taking advantage of economic downturns. For example, I once saw a sign suggesting people give up their office space and use a "virtual office" to save money, so the companies managing the virtual office space could be doing very well in an economic slump. And, think of how many bankruptcy attorneys made a killing in recent years when foreclosures and bankruptcies were at an all-time high in many communities. This is why you need to keep your finger on the pulse of the local business community. It will be important to know which businesses are doing well in your community, both for the approach to the business and to determine which business leaders have accumulated great wealth for themselves.

No matter what the economic situation is, you will need to be creative in your approach to the business community. You will need to try different approaches.

One of the reasons many nonprofits fail to inspire their local business community is because they are too unimaginative in their approach to businesses. Many nonprofits only talk to their local business community when they want them to sponsor another event. Yet, this is the one area of cooperate funding that decreased the most in recent years. Many businesses have established policies against corporate sponsorships of events. If a company is short-staffed because of layoffs, it most likely does not want to sponsor a golf tournament in which the business is expected to send four employees off for the day to play golf. The company might find it more trouble than it's worth to decide which employees should fill a table at a gala dinner dance, or to sponsor a team to walk, run,

## One Example of a Creative Approach

One organization dropped two of its four annual special events and approached the sponsors of these events to "adopt a family" served by the organization in lieu of their event sponsorship. At the end of the year they invited the companies' senior management to attend a dinner at which each of the company leaders sat with the family they sponsored. The families had each made a gift for the company that adopted them and told the management about the activities in which they had participated during the year, thanks to the sponsorship of this company. The corporate leaders all renewed their sponsorship for another year and many agreed to help find other sponsors so the organization could serve even more families next year.

**example**

dance or bowl on company time. Many communities are tapped out with events and the local business leaders would prefer sponsoring a program, where they can see their money being used to fund services, rather than paying for a band, a sumptuous meal or tee-shirts.

## Changes in the Way Corporations and Businesses Support their Nonprofit Community

In 2009, most businesses and corporations decreased their giving; however, there was an increase in both cash and in-kind gifts from large financial institutions and pharmaceutical companies, as well as an overall increase in in-kind gifts, which was sufficient enough to account for an overall increase in corporate giving. According to *Giving USA*, the bump in giving was in great part due to the increase in gifts-in-kind, which are more recession-proof than cash donations.

As stated previously, the area of corporate giving that showed the greatest decrease in both 2009 and 2010 was event sponsorships. Another interesting statistic shows that despite the increase from large financial institutions and pharmaceutical companies, if you look at giving from large companies opposed to giving from smaller companies, the smaller companies come out on top.

According to the Foundation Center, giving by the nation's approximately 2,700 grantmaking corporate foundations remained basically unchanged in 2010 at an estimated $4.7 billion. Corporate giving rose 10.6 percent from 2009 although, adjusted for inflation, this figure is 8.8. This is a significant increase in corporate giving; in fact, from 2008 to 2010, the increase is a whopping 23.2 percent (21.6 adjusted for inflation). Another exciting statistic shows that 65 percent of corporations increased their giving in 2010 over 2009.

In-kind gifts can be extremely helpful to many nonprofits, especially if the organization is engaged in a capital campaign. For example, one of my clients received approximately one-third of its campaign goal in gifts-in-kind, including paving of driveways and parking lots, cement used to construct the building furniture, computers, windows, tile and stone.

Other examples of gifts-in-kind could include:

◆ office supplies and furniture

◆ bed linens for a shelter

◆ medical supplies for a clinic

◆ kitchen supplies for a soup kitchen

◆ architectural services

◆ computer-technology equipment and services

◆ printing

◆ gift certificates that can be used as door prizes or silent auction items

◆ tickets to movies or events that could be given to families served by a human service agency

◆ accounting or legal services

◆ cleaning services

All of these changes in the way business gets done today indicate several things that nonprofit fundraisers need to keep in mind:

◆ Don't only approach your business community to sponsor events; this is the biggest area of decline in corporate funding.

◆ Don't forget about gifts-in-kind; they can be a recession-proof source of funding.

◆ Get rid of the "Willie Sutton Theory;" don't just look at the banks and big companies in your community. Approach some of the smaller companies.

Remembering the "Willie Sutton Theory," check your local and regional companies as well as the large national firms which might be based in or have offices or retail outlets in your community.

**Employee Involvement in Corporate Philanthropy**

In larger companies, there is a trend towards empowering their employees to make the giving decision and to get involved with

---

**The Willie Sutton Theory**

Willie Sutton was an infamous bank robber during the early part of the twentieth century. Someone once asked Willie why he robbed banks. His answer was simple: "That's where the money is!"

Nonprofits often get caught up in the Willie Sutton Theory, looking at the financial institutions and the big corporations in the community for funding since "that's where the money is." At least it appears so at first glance.

Please get yourself out of the Willie Sutton mentality and develop a list of smaller companies in your community, especially entrepreneurial ones that could be donors for your organization.

their local community organizations. One way to find out about the company's philosophy in this regard is to do some research on the Internet. A quick scan will show you that some large companies such as Microsoft, Macy's and Allstate have philosophies that encourage employees to get active in their communities. Some have employee-based foundations such as the MGM Voice Foundation, which allow employees to make decisions about where their donation will be allocated.

### Example of Microsoft's Employee Giving Program

At Microsoft, we believe that the passion and creativity of our employees emerge when they know their efforts make a difference—and a large part of that comes through helping others. We're proud of the fact that our employees make an extraordinary impact by engaging with their communities, and we have several programs in place to support their work.

*Giving Programs*

Like many companies in the United States, we match our employees' donations dollar for dollar. At Microsoft, we take it one step further by matching volunteer time at $17 per hour through the Volunteer Time Matching program. Through this benefit, the allocated limit is US $12,000 per employee, per year. International employees are provided a minimum of three days of paid time off to volunteer in their local communities.

◆ The Microsoft Employee Giving Campaign is held each October for employees in the United States, focusing on community awareness and fundraising.

◆ The year-round Microsoft matching gifts program matches U.S. employees' direct cash and software donations up to $12,000 annually to thousands of eligible 501(c)(3) and educational institutions.

◆ Similar matching gift programs are administered worldwide by participating subsidiaries.

*Volunteering Programs*

We support our employees' individual efforts to volunteer for causes that are meaningful to them.

◆ Microsoft time-matching programs encourage volunteerism in a variety of civic, environmental, and health and human services causes that the employee supports.

◆ Strategic community initiatives focus on mobilizing employees to support Microsoft Unlimited Potential and other programs operated by Microsoft strategic community partners, including NPower, United Way, HandsOn Network, and the Boys & Girls Clubs of America.

◆ Board service programs encourage employees to take on leadership roles with nonprofit agencies and to provide high-value business and technology consulting to their communities.

◆ Team-based volunteering events expose employees to community needs and inspire a longer-term relationship through community-wide service opportunities, such as the United Way's annual Day of Caring, and Seattle Works Day, sponsored by the Hands On Network.

◆ Disaster relief and humanitarian aid programs provide immediate help in a time of crisis. For example, Microsoft employee expertise and financial resources, combined with corporate financial and software donations, were powerful forces in the aftermath of the tsunami in Southeast Asia in 2004, Hurricane Katrina in 2005, and the China earthquake in 2008.

◆ Microsoft Volunteer Connection helps Microsoft employees in the U.S. connect to their local communities, find volunteer opportunities, and register volunteer hours for a cash match.

*United Way Loaned Executive Program*

The annual United Way Loaned Executive Program helps businesses in the Puget Sound area of Washington develop and carry out their yearly giving campaigns. Through the program, Microsoft and other companies loan some of their best and brightest employees from August through November to help with fundraising in the local community. The Microsoft Loaned Executives also contribute their talents internally for the Microsoft Giving campaign.

*Work with Microsoft Volunteers*

If you are part of a nonprofit organization and would like to post volunteer opportunities for Microsoft employees, you can do so on the Web sites for Idealist and the United Way of King County.

Many companies encourage their employees to volunteer for nonprofits, and often decisions to give or not give are based on whether the company's employees serve on boards or volunteer for the nonprofit requesting funding.

## Example of Employee Giving Program:

Welcome to the MGM Resorts Foundation

*Our employees are joining together to change lives in the communities where we live and work. The $6.9 million that employees donated to the Foundation in 2008 is a shining example of our commitment to making a difference. I am proud to be part of a team with so many people who are generous, compassionate, and dedicated to being part of the solution.*

*Together, we build stronger communities.*

Jim Murren
Chairman and Chief Executive Officer
MGM Resorts International

*MGM Resorts Foundation Mission*

> Through choice, we are empowered to build stronger communities where we live and work. We uplift lives, and create positive impact.

*The MGM Resorts Foundation*

> At MGM Resorts International, we know that every employee is an important part of their community and it's only natural that they want to make a difference and give something back.

> The MGM Resorts Foundation brings the best of our employee volunteer and charitable efforts together with greater impact and greater choice.

> Employee donations are recognized together with those of their co-workers as a part of the MGM Resorts International Foundation team.

> MGM Resorts International has its own public foundation, which focuses employee charitable contributions to nonprofit agencies and community organizations. This gives employees who support the foundation greater control and impact over their donations and the ability to support organizations in the communities we all live, work and care for our families.

*Offering more ways to care: The MGM Resorts Foundation*

> The MGM Resorts Foundation gives more ways to care.

> The Foundation invites employees to give through payroll pledge deductions or one-time contributions.

> ◆ Donations go farther because 100 percent of every dollar pledged goes directly to the charitable organization or cause designated.

> ◆ MGM Resorts International absorbs 100 percent of all administrative costs associated with donations. Our employees choose where their donations go.

> ◆ The Foundation Community Funds

> ◆ A specific charity of choice

- ◆ Their local United Way Affiliate

- ◆ Children's Medical Support Fund

- ◆ And, the Employee Emergency Relief Fund.

The choice belongs to each member of the MGM Resorts International team.

Together, we make a difference.

## Example of a Company Philanthropic Philosophy:

*The Foundation is committed to supporting the diverse communities in which NV Energy operates. We take this commitment very seriously by actively participating in communities in three ways: philanthropy, civic leadership and volunteerism. Giving back to the communities in which we operate makes them better places to live and work, and it turn makes them better places to do business.*

*We support our local communities through financial contributions as well as through community service. We measure our success through the eyes of our employees, our shareholders, our customers, our business partners and our neighbors. As active participants in communities in which we serve, we seek to understand and support emerging issues that are important to all our stakeholders.*

## Small Businesses and Entrepreneurs

As I've mentioned before, small businesses are actually more generous than large businesses. These small businesses are often run by entrepreneurs, the risk-takers, often financed by venture capital. These leaders are often forward-thinking enough to be attracted to a nonprofit that is visionary in its thinking.

While some people think of the classic entrepreneurs such as Bill Gates, Oprah Winfrey, or the founders of Ben and Jerry's, there are undoubtedly entrepreneurs in your own community, many of whom will be "under the radar" of other nonprofits in town. These could include bakery owners, Internet business operators,

> ### It's Not Always the "Big Guys" that Count!
>
> In 2009, Fortune 100 companies gave 10 percent of their gross revenue, while all companies gave 13 percent of their gross revenue.
>
> Fortune 100 companies gave $559 per employee, while all companies gave $650 per employee.
>
>  practical tip

farmers, media owners, sports franchise owners, restaurant owners, and many other examples. We will talk more in a future chapter about some of the types of businesses in your community you might want to identify and with which to build relationships. Your research should start by checking the list of businesses in your community that have a business license, obtaining a list of chamber of commerce members, searching the Internet, or just by driving around your community to find these businesses.

*What is small business and how many small businesses are there in the United States?*

In making a detailed definition, the Small Business Administration might use a number of criteria, including the number of employees, annual receipts, affiliates, or other applicable factors. The Office of Advocacy defines a small business for research purposes as an independent business having fewer than 500 employees. Firms wishing to be designated small businesses for government programs, such as contracting, must meet size standards specified by the U.S. Small Business Administration Office of Size Standards. Small businesses:

- ◆ Represent 99.7 percent of all employer firms.

- ◆ Employ just over half of all private sector employees.

- ◆ Pay 44 percent of total U.S. private payroll.

- ◆ Have generated 64 percent of net new jobs over the past fifteen years.

♦ Create more than half of the nonfarm private gross domestic product (GDP).

**Entrepreneur**

A person who organizes, operates, and assumes the risk for a business venture.

♦ Hire 40 percent of high tech workers (such as scientists, engineers, and computer programmers).

♦ Are 52 percent home-based and 2 percent franchises.

Companies of all sizes are looking for the bottom line impact in their community. In fact, some are very specific about the results expected. NV Energy, for example, states that it funds programs that can measure their performance. "Quality-of-life indicators define measurable program outcomes, and we encourage organization applying for grants to identify regionally specific quality of life indicators their organizations or program support, and the accompanying measurement of program success." In other words, businesses are interested in the bottom line, not just for their companies, but for the programs and organizations they support.

**To Recap**

♦ In order to successfully approach your business community you need to understand its concerns and needs. To do this, you first have to be where the business leaders are! Get to know your local business community leaders and ask for their advice before you ask them for money. Understand that they deal with the same issues you deal with every day—lack of sufficient staff, competition, an uncertain economy, and the challenge of keeping up with ever-changing technology.

♦ Try to offer businesses a variety of ways they can support your organization, including gifts-in-kind, matching gifts and multi-year pledges. During a time of recession you might have to be more creative in your approach to businesses.

◆ Remember to dispel the "Willie Sutton Theory" in your organization and don't always go to "the usual suspects." There is a whole world of new opportunity waiting for you if you talk to smaller companies, entrepreneurs, and some of the companies you might not have approached before.

# Chapter Four

## Why Businesses and Corporations Give

### IN THIS CHAPTER

···➔ What type of organizations receive money from businesses and corporations?

···➔ Why do businesses support some organizations and not others?

···➔ What can you do to get better results from your local business community?

In every community there are organizations that seem to always be in the news because some major corporation gave them a huge check or named a building in their capital campaign, while other organizations struggle to get local businesses to notice them. There are several reasons for this and the more you can learn from organizations that are getting corporate support, the more likely it is that your organization will someday be one of those newsmakers.

So why not ask those nonprofits what they doing right? Take the executive director or director of development to lunch and ask how they got started in their approach to businesses and what makes them successful.

Some questions you should ask in these advice-gathering sessions with nonprofit leaders include:

◆ How do you approach businesses for support?

◆ To what do you attribute your success with businesses?

◆ How do you identify which businesses have an interest in your organization?

◆ How do you involve corporate volunteers in your organization?

◆ What kind of fundraising materials have you found business leaders respond to?

Most likely you will hear some of these answers:

◆ We have someone from that company on our board.

◆ The company has been supporting us for years, and has increased its giving over time.

◆ We provided the company with something it needs/wants (recognition, a benefit to its employees, making our community a better place to live and work).

◆ We have a strong case for support and we presented it well.

### The Case for Support

First, you need to make sure your organization has a strong case for support that provides both emotional and rational reasons to give. Yes, business leaders do have emotions, just like anyone else, and the picture of the abandoned dog will appeal to a business leader who loves dogs. (I've seen a top hard-as-nails business executive cry at the thought of abandoned animals.) Or a story of a disabled young adult might resonate with a business leader who has a disabled person in her family (about one in ten of us do). But, just as with individuals, before a business leader will "write out the check" or get the company to consider the appeal, you need to show the rational side of your cause. What is the bottom line? How many people in the community are impacted by your program? (Chances are this company's employees will be among those people.) What are the measurable outcomes of your program?

In the book, *YOU and Your Nonprofit: Practical Advice and Tips from the CharityChannel Professional Community,* Contributing Authors Robert Penna and Ken Berger define outcomes as:

> *Above all else, the following should be your overall guide in identifying your outcomes:*
>
> ♦ *Good outcomes are best defined before the work, the project or the program begins. They are something you work toward, not something you try to identify amidst the confusion of all else that might have gone on or been done.*
>
> ♦ *A good outcome is not defined in terms of the absence of a problem.*
>
> ♦ *A good outcome is not defined merely in terms of the delivery of a service.*
>
> *Beyond this, good, well-defined outcomes, no matter what the subject or the area of an organization or program's focus, tend to share certain usually interrelated and mutually reinforcing characteristics. Among these are that the targeted goals are:*
>
> ♦ *Positive Improvements*
>
> ♦ *Meaningful*

- ◆ *Sustainable*

- ◆ *Bound in Time*

- ◆ *Bound in Number*

- ◆ *Narrowly Focused & Doable (with a stretch!)*

- ◆ *Measurable*

- ◆ *Verifiable.*

In his book, *The Nonprofit Outcomes Toolbox: A Complete Guide to Program Effectiveness, Performance Measurement, and Results,* Penna relates a story of how important outcomes measurement is to businesses.

Six Sigma is a management strategy used by a business to improve the quality of its products by decreasing defects during the manufacturing process. This concept has been used by those in the service industry and nonprofits as well although it is often unknown in the nonprofit world. In fact, I was in a meeting with one of my clients when a volunteer distributed her business cards with the designation "Green Belt" listed after her name. Someone commented that they never saw anyone list their Karate ranking on their business cards, until she explained the Six Sigma program's use of various color "belts" to define the competency of its users.

Penna reports that Easter Seals Iowa, after its use of several accepted types of nonprofit outcomes measurement seemed to leave corporate leaders cold, opted to use the Six Sigma method, a format with which its corporate donors were more familiar. After putting their outcomes in Six Sigma language, including a business case for each model, they reported not only nods of approval from the business leaders, but greatly-increased financial support.

## Transparency

Transparency is a key component of your ask to a business. Larry Seedig, president of USAA Bank, says one of things his company looks for is to make sure the organization is transparent. He wants to know its sources of funding and how the funds will be used, exactly how many people are affected by the organization's programs, and the demographics of those people.

Your 990 Form is one way to assure that your organization is transparent. Remember that companies wishing to invest in your organization might ask for your Form 990 or choose to search for it themselves on http://www.guidestar.org. So make sure your Form 990 is accurate and that it reflects well on your organization. The Form 990 does have a space in which you can describe your programs, so in addition to the treasurer or chief financial officer, the development office should have input into the preparation of this form. It can be a valuable public relations tool.

Another question you might hear from businesses is how your nonprofit is affected by and adheres to the Sarbanes-Oxley Act of 2002. While most of the bill does not relate directly to nonprofits, businesses will be more likely to support an organization that is

The Sarbanes–Oxley Act, sometimes called SOX, was passed into law as a result of corporate scandals which resulted in a loss of public confidence in both businesses and nonprofits. Most of the law does not apply to nonprofits, except for the document destruction and whistle-blower protection. However, many nonprofits have used the law to guide the improvement of their own reporting and transparency guidelines. One of the good results this law has had on the nonprofit community is that it has prompted many nonprofit boards to take governance more seriously, to implement strong financial committees, and to increase the professionalism of their financial reporting.

finition

following the same regulations that their business follows when it comes to transparency.

Remember that banks are required by law to contribute to their communities through the Community Reinvestment Act (CRA), so financial institutions are particularly interested in serving low-to-moderate-income people because that is what the CRA requires. Many community organizations will need to prove that their programs directly affect low-to-moderate income populations.

Other companies might be looking for the economic impact of your programs on the community. Some organizations have prepared an economic impact statement that includes statistics such as: How much it would cost if your clients were incarcerated instead of being treated in your programs, or how much money citizens will spend in a city with a performing arts center.

The following information from Americans for the Arts is a good example of how a nonprofit can make a strong case to the business community that the nonprofit sector has a positive economic impact on its community. Perhaps your industry has similar statistics you can use to make your case.

*Direct and indirect economic impact: How a dollar is re-spent in a community*

Arts & Economic Prosperity III uses a sophisticated economic analysis called input/output analysis to measure economic impact. It is a system of mathematical equations that combines statistical methods and economic theory. Input/output analysis enables economists to track how many times a dollar is "re-spent" within the local economy, and the economic impact generated by each round of spending. How can a dollar be re-spent? Consider the following example:

A theater company purchases a gallon of paint from the local hardware store for twenty dollars, generating the direct economic impact of the expenditure. The hardware store then uses a portion

Case Study in Economic Impact:

Several years ago Mom's House, Inc. prepared an economic impact statement showing the results of its program on the community. Here is an excerpt from its case for support:

> Mom's House was founded in Johnstown, PA in 1983 by Peg Luksik to offer young women with unplanned pregnancies a viable practical alternative to the despair of abortion and the tragedy of welfare. This unique program, the first of its kind in the nation, has served as a national model of private and public sector cooperation in dealing with the complex and growing dilemma of single parenthood.
>
> In its fifteen years of operation Mom's House has proven to be a practical and innovative approach to solving one of the most serious problems facing our society today. To date, the Mom's House system has brought hope and peace of mind to over 1,100 single parents and a chance for a better life to more than 1,300 children. Mom's House graduates are leading successful lives as teachers, nurses, engineers, attorneys, etc. More than 800 people have been removed from the welfare rolls as a direct result of their experience with the Mom's House program. In 1997 alone, Mom's House saved its communities over $8 million by moving people from welfare to working in a meaningful career. This figure does not include the money put back into the economy in the form of federal, state and local taxes paid by these new working people. Mom's House has proven over and over again that parents can choose life, that we can solve problems and that we can do it without any financial support from government.

stories from the real world

**Economic Impact of the Nonprofit Arts & Culture Industry (2005)**

(Expenditures by both organizations and audiences)

Total Expenditures $ 166.2 billion

Full-Time Equivalent Jobs 5.7 million

Resident Household Income $ 104.2 billion

Local Government Revenue $ 7.9 billion

State Government Revenue $ 9.1 billion

Federal Income Tax Revenue $ 12.6 billion

**observation**

of the aforementioned twenty dollars to pay the sales clerk's salary; the sales clerk re-spends some of the money for groceries; the grocery store uses some of the money to pay its cashier; the cashier then spends some for the utility bill; and so on. The subsequent rounds of spending are the indirect economic impacts.

Thus, the initial expenditure by the theater company was followed by four additional rounds of spending (by the hardware store, sales clerk, grocery store, and the cashier). The effect of the theater company's initial expenditure is the direct economic impact. The subsequent rounds of spending are all of the indirect impacts. The total impact is the sum of the direct and indirect impacts.

*Note:* Interestingly, a dollar "ripples" very differently through each community, which is why each study region has its own customized economic model.

*Audience Spending*

The arts and culture industry, unlike many industries, leverages a significant amount of event-related spending by its audiences. For example, a patron attending an arts event might pay to park the car in a garage, purchase dinner at a restaurant, eat dessert after the show, and return home to pay the babysitter. This generates related commerce for local businesses such as restaurants, parking garages, hotels, and retail stores. Total event-related spending by nonprofit arts and culture audiences was an estimated $103.1 billion in 2005. This spending supports 3.1 million full-time jobs in the United States, provides $46.9 billion in household income, and generates $16.4 billion in government revenue.

> *Mayors understand the connection between the arts industry and city revenues. Besides providing thousands of jobs, the arts generate billions in government and business revenues and play an important role in the economic revitalization of our nation's cities.*
>
> Douglas H. Palmer
> Mayor of Trenton, NJ
> President, The United States
> Conference of Mayors, 2005

Nationally, the typical attendee spends an average of $27.79 per person, per event, in addition to the cost of admission. Businesses that cater to arts and culture audiences reap the rewards of this economic activity.

*Impact of Nonprofit Arts & Culture Audiences*

◆ Total Expenditures $ 103.1 billion

◆ Full-Time Equivalent Jobs 3.1 million

◆ Resident Household Income $ 46.9 billion

◆ Local Government Revenue $ 5.1 billion

◆ State Government Revenue $ 5.6 billion

◆ Federal Income Tax Revenue $5.7 billion

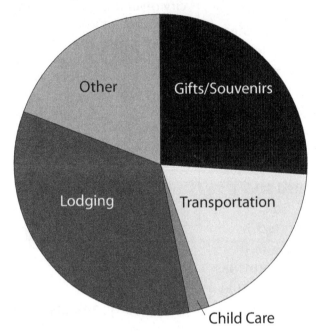

# Amount Spent Per $1 of Admission

Other

Gifts/Souvenirs

Lodging

Transportation

Child Care

Expenditures by Nonprofit Arts and Culture Organizations (2005). Nonprofit arts and culture attendees spend $27.79 per person above the cost of admission.

observation

## Presenting Your Case

A strong case for support is critical and you must know how to present this case to the business community. Most business leaders will not take the time to read information you send them in the mail and you probably will not be able to reach top business executives by phone. Getting past the gatekeeper is usually a huge hurdle. (I have found, however, that sometimes by calling at 7:30 a.m., an executive might be at the office well before the gatekeeper starts answering the phone. I've been successful in getting right to the top this way a number of times.) Getting to know the gatekeepers, however, is another good strategy to help you make contact with corporate leaders.

Business leaders say they respond better to a case if it is presented in a manner to which they can relate. Sometimes you might literally have the opportunity to use your elevator speech, so have it prepared. Know your case inside and out so if you do get into the elevator with the corporate CEO (I've actually had it happen to me) you can explain your case in thirty to sixty seconds, at least enough to pique the executive's interest. Have a one page fact sheet that you can hand or email to a business leader. A sample of a fact sheet is included in Appendix G. Develop a top-notch website that presents your case graphically and with a concise explanation of your programs.

Every nonprofit leader needs to know the organization's thirty-second "elevator speech." You never know when you will have a minute or less to make your case to a business leader, sometimes literally, in an elevator.

One museum planned a unique way to present its case to the business community. It prepared a one-page fact sheet and invited local business leaders to learn more about the museum by attending a "Breakfast Under the Stars." The event was held in the planetarium and, after a brief planetarium show, business leaders were given the fact sheet and an invitation to become a corporate sponsor or corporate "stars" of the museum.

### Benefit to the Company

The benefits to the company can be tangible or intangible. A Tower Perrins study found that corporate social responsibility is the third most important driver of employee engagement overall, proving that charitable activities affect the company's bottom line. However, for some companies, the leadership or the stockholders might be looking for more tangible, hard results of their community investments. In other words, there are some things that prompt companies to support the organizations that can 'deliver the goods.'

For example, organizations that provide a direct service that benefits the employees of the company will have a better chance of corporate support. Some examples of this might include:

◆ The local heart association providing a smoking cessation clinic for employees

◆ A drug and alcohol counseling center providing a program on teen drinking prevention for the company's employees

◆ Disease-related organizations providing information to employees on spotting Autism, Alzheimer's, etc.

◆ An art museum or zoo providing discounted memberships for employees

**Recognition**

During a capital campaign, recognition in the form on a named building or space within a building can be a motivating factor to support an organization. On a smaller level, having a company banner on the stage at an event, a sign on the golf course indicating the company's sponsorship of the tournament, or the company name listed in the newspaper can be an incentive to give. One university recognized corporate donors in its local business journal with a small ad that ran weekly featuring all its corporate supporters. This was a great place to recognize business donors, because other businesses saw the ad and wanted to be part of this great publicity.

While many individuals offer their gifts anonymously because they do not want to have every nonprofit in town contacting them, or because they shy away from public accolades, often for religious reasons, most businesses want to be publicly recognized as being good corporate citizens. Next time you walk into a corporate executive's office, take note of the recognition times displayed there. It will give you a good idea of what other nonprofits this company supports. It can also be a conversation starter and might give you some insight into what type of recognition items the executive is most impressed with. You might even ask, "Which of these items really means a lot to you and why?" It pays to know who your competition is. You might also find that the executive is proud of the company's community support and might even brag that this company gives more than its competitors.

In fact, there is often a level of competition among businesses of the same sector. This is generally thought to be one of the reasons that capital campaigns attract a higher percentage of corporate gifts than are included in the overall statistics showing how much money comes from foundations, corporations and individuals. Many companies will want to be certain that their company has a room or area bearing its name on a plaque, especially if their competitors are naming rooms in the same facility. Named gifts, whether a room or a program, are most effective when the naming opportunity fits the company's image. Some examples: the Microsoft Technology Learning Center, the Fisher-Price Children's Center, the Local Accounting Firm's Accounting Scholarship, and the ABC Landscaping Company Meditation Garden.

The basics of a good case for support are important when inviting businesses to make an investment in your organization,

---

### Competition often works in the corporate world

In one campaign, competition among banks worked to the advantage of the nonprofit. At a campaign cabinet meeting, in which the heads of four local banks were in attendance, a banker was bragging to one of his competitors that his bank was four times the size of the other banker's institution. "Oh good," said the competing banker, "we're giving $100,000 to the campaign, so I guess you will be contributing at least $400,000."

**stories from the real world**

whether for annual support, capital campaigns or special projects. A case checklist can be found in Appendix F to help you check whether your case is effective or not.

### Establishing the Relationship

Just as with individuals, companies need first to be introduced to your organization and to be cultivated over the years before they are ready to make a significant investment in your organization. Business leaders who were recently surveyed responded that they very seldom make a large gift to an organization without which they have some type of relationship. They might be vendors to the organization, or perhaps they are neighbors of the organization. They might use the organization's services, or have a natural affiliation with the organization. Most of the time, the company executives have been cultivated by the organization and have become enthused about its programs and services. We'll talk more about building relationships in a future chapter.

---

### An enterprising idea

One organization, while preparing its case for support, struggled with the concept of whether or not it could request named gifts for rooms or areas that were already named but were now in need of renovation.

It had a good opportunity to solve this issue. One local bank had sponsored a room within the facility a number of years prior to this campaign. The bank had been involved with a merger and now had a different name. Representatives went to the bank and proposed that it fund the renovation of this room, promising a new plaque that had the bank's current name. Several other donors then agreed to name rooms if they could have new plaques placed in the rooms they sponsored.

**stories from the real world**

## Involving Corporate Leaders in Your Organization

The best way to solidify relationships with the company is to get its leaders involved with your organization. Being invited to serve on a board, an advisory committee or serving as a volunteer in other ways is one reason most business leaders say they feel inspired or even obligated to make a gift from their company. Other ways you can involve business leaders is to invite them to serve on a capital campaign cabinet, an ad hoc committee or a prospect identification screening session. Or you can involve them directly in your programs. Inviting business leaders to serve as mentors to your young clients, read to students, serve on a technology advisory committee, etc. are just a few examples of how you can involve business leaders in your organization.

It will be important to research and understand the company's giving priorities before approaching them.

## Why do Some Organizations Succeed and Others Fail in Reaching the Business Community?

Organizations succeed in raising money from businesses because they know how to work with their business community. Those nonprofits that are not successful in raising money from their local business community have usually not learned the secrets to working with businesses. They will use the wrong methods of approach, approach the wrong people, not understand the company's giving policies, or not appropriately recognize the company.

## Some Ill-Advised Approaches to Businesses

Many nonprofit organizations can't seem to figure out why their local business communities are not supporting them financially. There are several answers to this question:

◆ The organization does not understand that companies are in business to make money, not to be philanthropic.

♦ The organization has not built relationships with the business community.

♦ The organization uses the wrong methods to approach businesses.

Let's address each of these issues.

*Operating from an "entitlement" mentality*

Some organizations assume that businesses "owe them" support. I recall one executive director of a human service agency who not only embarrassed herself and her organization, but ended up losing her job, because of this perception.

Her organization was applying for a grant and she and her board chair met with the review committee consisting of the community's leading corporate executives. After being denied the grant, she proceeded to express her feelings in a very unprofessional outburst in the reception area of the funder's place of business. The board chair, after reporting the incident to the executive committee, urged them to replace this executive director. The full board voted on her removal shortly after, replacing her with a more professional director.

Another organization had rejected a bid from a contractor, not because of a more competitive bid, but because the facilities director had a personal relationship with the competing contractor. The development director, unaware that this unfair practice had taken place, called on the contractor who had lost the bid, and asked for a gift. The executive director could not understand why this contractor did not want to make a gift to the organization. She felt that the organization deserved support and even hinted that this contractor should give so he could be considered for future projects. Not only unprofessional, but unethical behavior!

*Not understanding the corporate mindset*

Many large organizations, such as colleges and universities, for some reason, lump together businesses with foundations and set up a Corporate and Foundation Gifts department within their development offices. The two entities are very different and, therefore, the approaches to them must be very different. Foundations are in business to give away money; corporations are in business to make money for their stockholders. It's as simple as that! Even the local business owner, who is a sole proprietor, partnership or a privately held corporation, although not being accountable to stockholders as is a publicly held corporation, has set up business with the idea of showing a profit. This is sometimes a simple concept that nonprofits find hard to grasp, particularly if most of their

---

## A classic example of using the wrong approach

One nonprofit had a development staff composed of people who had all come from a human service background and none of whom had a business background. They organized an appeal to ask for contributions from local businesses by involving a committee of business leaders who would contact other businesses in the community. They started the meetings at 9 a.m. and ended them around 11 a.m. and were disappointed in the attendance at these meetings. However, they found an easy solution. One of the corporate volunteers asked the chief development officer if she could share with him some of her ideas to improve the meetings. The first suggestion she made was to move the meetings from 9 a.m. to 7:30 a.m. and assure participants that they would be out of these meetings by 8:30 a.m. A simple adjustment but it resulted in a 100 percent increase in attendance! Some of the other suggestions from this businesswoman were: to create a case for support that showed the bottom line impact of the organization on its community, have a business leader chair the meetings rather than the development officer, and to shorten the length of the time commitment asked of business leaders. All these suggestions were implemented and the program was a huge success.

stories from
the real world

previous fundraising efforts have been focused on grants. But it is a lesson that needs to be learned.

Does all of this mean that businesses are uncharitable, or selfish? No, they are a viable part of every community, creating jobs, bringing tourists or other businesses into the community, and generating tax revenues. Remember, most people, including business owners, care very deeply about their communities. Many businesses are extremely socially conscious, and even those that are not as altruistic will often give to nonprofits because of the direct or indirect benefit to their company or their employees, or because it helps them gain exposure or increase their market share.

*Using direct mail to approach businesses*

Many nonprofits take the approach of joining their local chamber of commerce and then once they join, request mailing labels for all the members and send out a mail appeal to chamber members. This method usually results in zero dollars or perhaps one or two responses. The reasons? The decision makers never get to see the request. It is not a personal approach. Most business leaders do not respond to direct mail for purchases, donations, even resumes

---

**Be careful when using direct mail**

One of the worst examples of this common mistake happened to me when I received a letter from a charity that had obviously purchased the local chamber list, of which my company was a member. Since many business owners were male, the charity assumed all were. I received a letter requesting a donation addressed on the outside envelope to Ms. Linda Lysakowski; inside was a form letter, with the salutation, "Dear Sir." Needless to say, they did not get a gift from my company.

**watch out!**

---

of prospective employees, or anything else. You need to make a personal contact with business leaders.

**A Great Way to Help Your Business Community, Your Nonprofit, and Yourself!**

When I was a development officer I made sure my organization not only joined the local chamber of commerce, but supported my efforts to get involved with the chamber. I attended all the breakfast meetings, mixers and events of the chamber. I volunteered to help with the chamber's annual membership drive. During this drive, chamber members spent two weeks contacting local businesses who were not yet chamber members and invited them to join. As I called on my assigned prospects, I handed them my business card and, of course, this almost always led to a conversation about my organization. I ended up with some great volunteers and corporate donors as a result. It was really a win-win-win situation. The chamber got new members. My organization gained more awareness, volunteers and money. The companies who joined the chamber, learned about how to better promote and manage their businesses. And, as a bonus, one year I won first prize in the membership drive and got dinner for two at a very exclusive restaurant in the area!

stories from the real world

Do not make the mistake of going to your local chamber of commerce and asking for the list of all its members for the purpose of sending a direct mail appeal. Your local chamber can be very helpful in identifying local business and if you get active in your chamber, this is a great way to build relationships with the business community. Likewise, local service clubs such as Rotary, etc., can help you find local business owners that you can involve in your organization. However, do not think the chamber or the service club is just a place to build your list of people to send your annual mail appeal. Most business people do not read the mail they receive from nonprofits. In fact, the mail is usually screened by a secretary or assistant who tosses it in the trash before it even lands on the owner's desk.

*The fallacy of the corporate/foundation relations office*

Major educational institutions often make the mistake of having a corporate/foundation relations officer or officers. In many cases these development officers are experienced in researching and writing grant proposals to foundations, but they do not have the skills to build relationships with businesses and corporations. Foundations are in the business of giving away money. The decisions they have to make involve which organizations best meet the interests of the foundation and has proven it can produce positive outcomes. On the other hand, businesses are in business not to give money away, but to make money for their owners or stockholders. The decisions businesses make, although they involve some of the same decisions foundations face, begin with whether or not they even want to give money away! So you first have to assess the philanthropic interests of the company and its leadership. Often, staff who work in the corporate/foundation relations office have good skills that can be helpful to research foundations and write proposals, but might not be the right people to approach businesses because they have never worked in the business community.

*Staff-driven appeals*

One organization that had a very successful annual business and corporate appeal involving hundreds of volunteers found that its results dropped dramatically after a change of administration. It was decided that the staff could manage this program on its own and it didn't need to involve volunteers in this effort. It decided to save its volunteers for capital campaign asks. As a result, the organization's annual giving from businesses dropped by more than 50 percent when solicitations were limited to those done by the chief development officer with help from the chief financial officer.

This situation is not that uncommon; many organizations involve volunteers in capital campaigns knowing that the in-person solicitation by a peer is always the most effective way to raise major gifts from both individuals and businesses. Unfortunately, after the campaign ends, many of these organizations do not keep these volunteers actively involved. Often the subsequent appeals to their businesses drop back to a mail appeal, or perhaps a phone call. Sometimes, the companies are not even asked to support annual giving. What a shame!

Staying in touch with donors on a regular basis, and keeping them updated on the progress of the campaign and the project, are important. Inviting all donors to the dedication and open house when the new facility is completed are steps that sometimes get overlooked. But remember, the key to successful fundraising is relationships, relationships, relationships; so, in order to build these good relationships the organization needs to maintain good donor communications.

Like donors, campaign volunteers will have developed more awareness and commitment to the organization. Keeping campaign volunteers involved in the organization's ongoing development efforts can be a real boost to fundraising efforts. Volunteers can help in the annual fund, major gifts programs, and planned giving campaigns, especially those who have been involved in making personal solicitations. They will have the training to become effective fundraisers because of their involvement in the campaign. Some of these volunteers might also be invited to serve on the board or the development committee.

*Approaching the wrong person*

Remember what we said earlier about research!

Many organizations fail because they approach the wrong person. I recall when my company joined the local chamber of commerce, I was allowed to list two staff people in its directory as a result of the size of my company. I listed myself (the business owner) and a gentleman who worked for me, as the contacts for the business. We got many calls based on this listing, but the calls usually were asking for the man whose name was listed. I recall taking several phone calls in which I answered the phone and the person on the other end insisted on talking to the "man in charge." These callers would have been much more successful if their approach had not been one of assuming that I was the assistant and the man whose name was listed owned the company. Never make assumptions!

Another assumption is to call the corporate giving office in larger companies. Although this office might handle the written solicitations and the details of contributions, it might not make the ultimate decision. It could be an employee committee or the CEO that makes the final decision. Get to know who the *real* decision makers are.

*Not being sensitive to the time of the decision maker*

You got the appointment. Congratulations! Now, don't blow it! Usually, getting the appointment is the hardest part of the whole deal. But, what do you spend so much time on? What you're going to do once you're in the door. Be careful. You might just kill the whole deal if you handle this part incorrectly. I've seen many nonprofits that finally get that important appointment with a potential funder and then come ill-prepared. They have too much information or not enough. They assume the business leaders understand the jargon of their industry. They ramble on and on, insensitive to the fact that this business leader has calls waiting, another meeting coming up, and a stack of emails to return.

## Some Better Approaches

*The "Cause Célèbre" Factor*

Many nonprofits are successful because they have recruited a celebrity spokesperson or some famous personage who is willing to either serve as a spokesperson or even to 'roll up their sleeves' and get intimately involved. Think about the Hurricane Katrina incident and the many stars that came to the aid of New Orleans, including Brad Pitt. Many famous 'stars' helped put the cause of AIDS organizations on the map. And if you think of giving to an animal rights group, you might have been influenced by a variety of people from Sarah McLaughlin to Bob Barker who have made animals their "cause célèbre."

Celebrities are not always movie stars or nationally recognized figures. Every community has its own 'stars.' Some nonprofits have been able to succeed in approaching the local business community because they have been successful in recruiting a 'champion' who a well known and respected leader in the community.

One organization was successful in making a name for itself in the local business community using the cause célèbre factor. The organization had a small board of eight very committed, but relatively unknown, people. One of the board members, however, was determined to put this organization "on the map." He pursued three of the top community business leaders inviting them to join the board. His first 'target' was the most successful and respected business owner in the community. He met with this business leader and convinced him to join the board. This charismatic business leader was responsible for then recruiting several other top business leaders in the area, including the president of the largest bank in that community and the chair of the largest manufacturing company in the area. With the support of these three leaders the organization was also successful in getting the publisher of the local newspaper on the board and several other well-known and respected leaders. The board grew to thirty-three members and, through the business contacts of these board members, it was successful in raising more than $350,000 in its very first annual appeal.

Another organization was successful in recruiting the CEO of its community's largest company to head its capital campaign. This 'celebrity' had so much influence in the community that instead of recruiting campaign cabinet members by the accepted method of a personal approach, they sent a letter to all the business leaders whom they wanted to recruit. This CEO's signature on the letter was enough to obtain the agreement of every person they invited to join the cabinet, including the presidents of the community's four largest banks.

## Build the Relationship First

*Asking for Advice*

Remember the saying I talked about earlier: If you want advice, ask for money; if you want money, ask for advice.

This old adage is especially true when it comes to raising money from your local business community.

Be careful though! One mistake some organizations make is starting an advisory committee and then wondering why this group is not helping them raise money. Often, organizations will succeed in getting some big corporate names on the letterhead by asking them to serve in an advisory capacity, but unless there is a clear job description that outlines the expectation as helping with fundraising, this group is going to think all you want is advice. There is a time to ask for advice, but there is also a time to ask for more involvement.

One public library needed to expand its reach into the community and raise more money. Its nine board members were politically appointed and, for the most part, were not interested in fundraising or public relations. They thought about starting an advisory committee that could help them with public relations and fundraising. However, after a consultant advised them that if they called it an advisory committee, its members would think they were only there to give advice (and they had plenty of that from the board), they decided to look for an alternative title for the group of business leaders they planned to invite to join. They settled on calling this group the Community Development Council. Something as simple as the right title and a job description that clearly outlined the role of this group as creating good public awareness and raising funds made all the difference in the world. Within the first year, the Community Development Council hosted a successful fundraising event, "Murder at the Library," created a Library Day that drew thousands of people, initiated a successful direct mail appeal, and ran a successful business appeal.

stories from
the real world

## To Recap

◆ Know the business community and learn what each company's funding priorities are before you approach it. Invite employees, especially key management, to get involved in your organization.

◆ Show the economic and social impact of your organization on the community.

◆ Don't make the mistake of using a nonprofit mindset to approach businesses. Avoid institutional jargon. Schedule meetings at convenient times for businesses. Recruit some local celebrities to help you. Know when you want advice and when you want more involvement from business leaders and make it clear what you are asking from these business leaders. Learn who the decision makers are and how to approach them.

# Chapter Five

## Getting Started: Identifying Business Prospects

### IN THIS CHAPTER

- ···→ Who are your best prospects for business and corporate gifts?
- ···→ Researching your local business community
- ···→ Moving beyond the "Willie Sutton Theory"
- ···→ Determining linkages, ability and interest

Remembering the statistics about the percentage of profits smaller companies give to charity and the "Willie Sutton theory," it will be to your advantage to find some of the smaller companies in your community and develop relationships with the leaders of these companies. Here are some examples of the types of companies that might be "under the radar" for other nonprofits in your community.

### Architectural firms

For many nonprofit organizations the word "architecture" conjures up images of futuristic buildings and gleaming, lacquered interiors.

**Architects Help Nonprofits Build Their Missions**

The Carrollton-Hollygrove Community Development Corporation, in New Orleans, was created to help residents rebuild their homes after Hurricane Katrina. Later, the nonprofit began to focus on the availability of fresh produce in the low-income neighborhood. Cordula Roser Gray, a local architect, worked with the group to develop a plan for a farmers market on a one-acre plot with an existing building. Demonstration gardens along the street help draw local residents into the twice-weekly farmers market and the group's gardening and cooking workshops.

stories from the real world

A new book, *The Power of Pro Bono*, seeks to dispel charities' misconceptions about design and show that it can be an important tool to help them advance their missions.

"There is a mentality in the nonprofit sector that we need to look needy, that we need to not be flashy," says John Cary, editor of the book.

Architectural firms can be especially helpful if your organization has capital needs. You do need be cautious, however, that an architect who donates preliminary drawings is not developing a concept that your organization cannot afford once you get into the construction phase.

*Developers*

Developers are often under the radar screen because they might not be active in civic and professional groups. They often travel a lot and are busy managing their companies. They usually operate under names that you might not recognize immediately but because of the many holdings they have, they are often quite successful.

One organization was able to develop a relationship with a young developer who owned several strip malls, office buildings, and other holdings. They were able to secure donated office space through this developer, as well as a significant personal gift from the developer.

He really believed in the mission of the organization and wanted to help. Although he was too busy to serve on their board, he was willing to meet with the board chair about once a month, review names of prospective donors, and make a few contacts for the organization with potential donors. He maintained his low profile, but was still able to help the organization achieve its financial goals.

*Technology companies*

All the hi-tech companies are not in Silicon Valley! Just about every community is home to one or more companies in the field of technology. In my own community, for example, two of the sixteen highest paid executives as reported in the local *Business Journal* are CEOs of technology companies.

As with developers, these entrepreneurs are often very busy and might not have time to get involved in civic and professional groups, or with your organization. But if you can get a contact to open the door to these businesses you might find it profitable.

---

**An architectural dream gone up in smoke**

One organization, a human service agency, engaged an architect to do a rendering of a new building. While it was looking for land on which to build the new facility, it engaged a consultant to do a planning study to test the feasibility of this project in the community. The building the architect designed was quite elaborate including a curved exterior wall which would be quite expensive. As the consultant conducted interviews, many of those interviewed expressed concern about the grandeur of this building for a human service organization that did most of its work in the community, not in a central location. One bank president studied the floor plan and then looked around his office and said to the consultant, "The executive director's office is larger than my office! Is all this really necessary for this type of organization? They might be better off just leasing space."

**watch out!**

---

One organization served the child of a high-tech industry leader and so was able to tap into this company's high profits and matching gift program. So make sure you know the people you serve and what contacts might be available through them.

*Transportation & moving industries*

This is one of those 'unglamorous' businesses that often gets overlooked in favor of the more high-profile companies such as financial institutions, utilities, and pharmaceutical companies. However, don't overlook any trucking companies, small airlines, bus companies, or moving companies that might be in your community.

One small airline owned a fleet of small planes used in the tourist industry. This company was so successful that its owner paid cash every time he bought a new plane. And yet, this business owner's name did not show up on any of the "usual suspect" lists.

Another organization was located in a community where there were two large trucking companies headquartered. During the planning phase of a capital campaign, the owner of one of the trucking companies was interviewed and agreed to serve on the campaign cabinet as well as secure a significant gift from his company. He was also able to open the door to the owner of his chief competitor. Although they were business rivals, they were good friends.

So even if you don't have a major airline based in your home town, don't forget some of the other transportation companies that might be in your neighborhood.

*Service industries*

There are numerous other industries that provide services such as pest control, maid service, food service, health care, beauty and personal care such as spas, and many more. These groups might not be housed in large, magnificent offices since their work is done off-site in many cases, but could be very profitable.

One health clinic received significant donations from a for-profit retirement community based in its city. A human service agency that dealt with developmental disabilities was the favorite charity of a vending company owner because his neighbor received services from this agency. And a local arts center received major support from the owner of a chain of beauty shops. These are just a few

## Don't judge a book by its cover!

You probably heard this from your mother or your kindergarten teacher, but it is so true.

Here are some instances that I have found of those quiet millionaires who were involved in an "unglamorous business."

◆ A board member of a human service agency who came to board meetings and barely ever said a word. She was a quiet woman who, along with her husband, owned and operated several car washes. The result of her involvement on the board: the largest gift and the first planned gift this organization ever received.

◆ A board chair, a builder, who always wore a plaid flannel shirt and a baseball cap. His gift, also the largest his organization ever received, led to a successful capital campaign for his organization.

◆ The owner of a very successful retail operation picked me up for a meeting one day in his Ford station wagon. Probably the wealthiest person in his community and one of the most generous.

◆ A retired farmer who, in his nineties, came to a church camp and sawed wood as his volunteer activity. He was also the largest donor to this group's capital campaign.

◆ And, my personal favorite, although not exactly a fundraising example: the woman who walked into the bank where I worked. I assumed she was homeless because she was carrying two large paper shopping bags. I got the surprise of my life when she proceeded to dump ten thousand dollars in cash on my desk to open a certificate of deposit.

stories from the real world

examples of service industries that are probably in your community and might not be tapped by every charity in town.

*Entertainment*

Virtually every community has movie theaters, for-profit art galleries, go-kart racetracks, golf and miniature golf courses, and numerous other places where people spend their entertainment dollars. Almost every state in the country now has casinos that are highly regulated and motivated to give charitable contributions.

Look around your community. Ask your staff, board and clients where they spend their entertainment dollars. Look for ways to create win-win situations with these businesses—perhaps offering tickets to your clients, or hosting events at their facilities, etc. Do your research to find out who the owners of these companies are so you can approach them personally for a more significant gift.

The list of businesses you can approach goes on and on, including everything from paper companies to refuse haulers, and even rag companies. (One of the most profitable businesses in one community in which I worked literally was a rag company.) Remember that Willie Sutton theory and don't just focus on the 'big guys.'

## The Quiet Millionaire

In their groundbreaking book, *The Millionaire Next Door*, Thomas J. Stanley and William D. Danko cite that 75 percent of millionaires are business owners. Many of their businesses are not glamorous (paving contractors, welding contractors, auctioneers, rice farmers, pest controllers, owners of mobile home parks, etc.).

Now, many of us probably don't have a rice farmer in our community, but we probably all have welding contractors, paving contractors, pest control companies and many of the other "unglamorous" businesses. So start making a list of some of the 'under the radar' businesses in your community. And then do your research on the companies and their owners.

**To Recap**

◆ The first step in any solicitation process is identifying potential donors. It is no different in the business world. You need to set aside some time to do research. Get your local chamber of commerce listing. Read the local *Business Journal*. Talk to your vendors. Look at donor lists of other nonprofits.

◆ Ask your board staff and clients about companies they do business with. Do some brainstorming with your board and development committee to find out who knows whom.

◆ Drive around your community and see what businesses are in your city, town, or even your neighborhood.

◆ Don't forget that every community has small and medium sized businesses and most have a few large businesses although they might not be the obvious ones you would look for. Find out if these companies are the headquarters or branch offices that might have discretionary finds.

◆ You have to be where the business leaders are! Get involved in your local chamber of commerce and other civic and professional organizations. Meet the business leaders where they are, and speak their language. Join your local chamber, civic and professional clubs and get to the meetings.

# Chapter Six

## Getting Started: Cultivation Strategies

### IN THIS CHAPTER

···→ Asking for advice (again)

···→ Cultivation events

···→ Cultivation activities

So, how do we know what motivates our local businesses to give to charitable causes? Ask them! Asking for the advice of the local business leader before asking for money is one of the keys to success. And, like all fundraising, corporate and business fundraising is built on the three key words in fundraising: relationships, relationships, relationships.

### Asking for Advice

There are several ways to involve the local business community in your organization's mission. One way is the one-on-one advice-giving session. Here are a few examples that have worked well.

In a recent survey I found that some creative ways of approaching corporations include these from Joanne Oppelt, MHA, GPC of CONTACT We Care, Inc.:

> ***Real Life Story I.*** *In 2005, I started a concerted effort to reach out to area banks to increase funding through Community Reinvestment Act (CRA). One of the banks I contacted was a small community bank located in the same municipality as my agency.*
>
> *At the same time, our agency held three mortgages totaling about $800,000 at 5.5 percent. The executive director had been trying for about two years to refinance the loans at a below market interest rate through a program related investment or like vehicle; the market was then hovering around 6 percent.*
>
> *I got a meeting with the president of the bank and introduced our agency to him, told him what we were about, discussed our business banking needs and what other opportunities to partner might be available. I told him too that I was approaching many banks in the area. The meeting lasted about forty-five minutes, and he said he would get back to me.*
>
> *A couple of weeks later, he asked me back. He told me he wanted to help our constituents with some of their emergency loan and financial literacy needs. He wanted to set up a revolving loan fund at no cost to our agency with a minimal interest rate for clients. I told him that was a great idea; in fact, such a great idea that we had already instituted such a program twenty years before. What would really help was to refinance the three loans we had outstanding. The money that we would save in interest would then be reinvested directly into funds set aside specifically for constituents.*
>
> *He asked the current terms of the loans and what I was looking for. I told him and said that I was trying to get the best deal for CAU that I could. I asked for 2 percent over ten years. He said that would cost him money and he wouldn't be able to do that but still wanted to help us. We talked for a while and settled on $800,000 at 4 percent over ten years with no closing costs, 2 percent below*

*market rate and 1.5 percent below the current terms. The deal saved our agency about $250,000 over the life of the loan.*

*We made the deal and were diligent in terms of repayment.*

*A number of months later, the bank president called me back in and said he was interested in having the bank make a charitable contribution to our agency. I asked what type of program he was interested in supporting and he said whatever we thought would be of most benefit to the agency and constituents. I asked in what amount and he said $10,000. He said we were the bank's charity of choice.*

*The bank has been a staunch supporter of ours ever since. The president has offered us other below market rate interest loans on other properties we have acquired. And the annual charitable contribution continues.*

***Real Life Story II.*** *I met the Director of Community Relations of a local utility company through an educational forum for arts agencies that the utility company sponsored. For two years, I pursued a relationship. I had joined the Regional Chamber of Commerce and Employer's Legislative Committee, and would run into this business leader at these events. I always followed up with a phone call or note on how good it was to see him.*

*Finally, we went to lunch and discussed the process for obtaining charitable funding from the company. I followed the procedures, and, viola, I got a donation! I was surprised to even get that far, as it took two years of persistence to even get the lunch date.*

*Now we have a relationship where I call him in September of each year to get on his charitable giving docket and he tells me the due dates of the paperwork.*

*Two years of hard work well spent.*

***Real Life Story III.*** *I met James at a real estate networking event and invited him to my agency's Community Network.*

*(The network is a group of area business representatives that meet twice a year that I had initiated to increase support for my agency's mission.) He attended the networking event and said he was interested in helping us out. It turned out that he was a representative for an energy supply company. After checking out our options, we decided to give it a try. We have saved thousands of dollars in our energy bills since then.*

*James also turned out to be a board member of a charity assisting needy people with furniture needs. This charity has since made contributions to our agency.*

## Cultivating Business Leaders

There is no substitute for one-on-one cultivation activities. It does take time but, as you can see from some of these examples, it's more than worth the effort.

Another great way to involve your local business leaders is to invite them to attend a "focus group," or business leaders' breakfast, where you are providing them with information about your organization and then asking for their input. The key to successful business gathering of this type is the invitation process. Ask a prominent local business leader with whom you already have an established relationship to host this event and invite his friends and peers to attend a brief breakfast meeting. Provide the host with a list of business leaders you would like to involve and ask the host to add to it. Generally breakfast meetings are best for business people so they can arrive early (perhaps 7 a.m. or 7:30 a.m.) and still get into their places of business by 8:30 or 9 a.m. Do not have the meeting run more than an hour and fifteen minutes. Inviting about twenty-five to thirty people will usually result in attendance of about a dozen or so business people. If possible, take them for a brief tour of your facility or a "virtual tour" by video or PowerPoint. Have one of the people you serve talk about your organization and what your organization means to them. Then invite the participants to have an open discussion, soliciting their advice on questions such as:

◆ How to better market your organization's services

◆ How to improve your fundraising program

◆ How they might be able to partner with your organization in some way

You can either give them a *brief* form to complete or have someone taking careful notes of the discussion. You will not be asking for money at this event, but for their advice!

> ***Real Life Story I.*** *A local emergency shelter wanted to embark on an annual corporate appeal; however, most of the community really didn't understand the organization's full range of services. One of the board members, the president of a local bank, agreed to talk to the CEO of a large manufacturing firm in the city. This CEO agreed to host a cultivation event for local business leaders so they could become more familiar with the shelter and its mission. He agreed to review the suggested invitation list and added a few names to the list. While preparing for the event, we invited the host to come take a tour himself. The more involved he became with the shelter, the more enthused he became. He agreed to send out the invitation letter on his letterhead and said his office would even handle printing and mailing the letters that the development office had written. The letter clearly stated that this was not a fundraising event and that the attendees would not be asked to contribute that day. We had anticipated that inviting seventy-five business leaders would result in about twenty attending. We were delighted that we had close to sixty business leaders attend that morning, due to the perceived importance of the invitation from the host.*
>
> *The event was a 7:30 a.m. breakfast and the invitation clearly stated that we would end by 8:45 a.m. The host first welcomed guests and told them how impressed he had been as he learned more about the many services of the shelter which included much more than providing a bed for the night, but extended to day care for homeless children, training in resume and job interview skills,*

medical and dental clinics, and more. The executive director of the shelter then thanked everyone for coming, gave a brief history of the shelter, and expanded on the number of people served by the shelter and told the group how the shelter was funded. The participants all understood the work of the shelter much better after this informal breakfast meeting.

The piece d 'resistance, however, was a tour of the shelter led by a former shelter guest, who showed the business leaders around the shelter, pointing out, "I used to sleep in that bed in the corner. Now I have a job at the shelter, my own apartment and am getting my life together." Several of the business leaders attending were so moved by this experience, they wanted to write out a check on the spot. However, the organization said, "No, we told you we would not ask for money at this event, and we are very serious about our promise. But, rest assured, we will be contacting you at a later time!"

When these business leaders were later approached for the annual appeal, they responded very generously because they now had a deep personal connection to the organization. At least a dozen of those who had attended the event volunteered to speak to other business leaders about their commitment to the shelter as well.

***Real Life Story II.*** *A drug and alcohol counseling center wanted to involve business leaders in its work. This group planned a breakfast for business and political leaders in its community. About seventy people attended. As with the shelter mentioned above, they had a business person host the event, welcome the guests and then asked the executive director to talk about the agency. They had two persons who gave brief testimonials. One was a judge who talked about how much money this organization saved taxpayers because it provided services that kept people out of the court system and helped them build new lives. She made quite an impressive presentation on the rational side of the case. As in the case of the shelter, this organization had an employee who had been a former client of the center and she gave a vivid testimonial about how the agency had helped change her life.*

*Again, an emotional and rational appeal helped present the agency's case to the business community.*

*At the end of the breakfast, brief questionnaires were distributed asking how the organization might partner with the companies represented. When the questionnaires were collected and reviewed, the organization had found a volunteer to design the agency newsletter, a company that agreed to print and mail the newsletter for them, and several people who indicated they would be interested in serving on the development committee to help the organization raise funds.*

***Real Life Story III.** Another homeless shelter held a fantastic cultivation event for mid-level managers of a large bank in their community. They targeted one company at a time for which they would host an event. At this particular event, as with others they held, the business leaders were invited to breakfast with the shelter guests. They sat at the same tables and shared a meal with the shelter guests. After breakfast the executive director took the business leaders on a brief tour and showed them first-hand the need for more space. But the thing that stuck in the minds of these potential funders was that they had shared a meal with someone who needed their help.*

***Real Life Story IV.** A human service agency that had developed their first-ever case for support wanted to test the case to see if would be compelling to the local business community. The chair of the development committee invited several business leaders to come to the agency for a luncheon to which he treated the guests. After lunch the host welcomed people and explained that, as indicated in the letter of invitation, they would not be asked for money, but simply for advice. The executive director talked briefly about the history and needs of the organization, and the development director presented the case for support which had been put into a PowerPoint format. After viewing the presentation, the host asked the guests what they thought of the case. "Were there parts that seemed more urgent than others? Was there anything they would eliminate, or add? How did they think the case should*

*be presented to businesses?" And the final question, "If you were
asked to contribute to this organization, would this case prompt
you to make a gift?"*

*The organization gained some valuable input from these business
leaders and saved a lot of money by not printing something
that might not tell an accurate story or be compelling enough to
prompt a gift.*

These are just a few examples of how successful organizations have
learned to build relationships and ask for advice before asking for
money.

Most organizations that try this approach leave the event with at
least one or two leads of local business leaders who want to develop
a further relationship with the organization. Make sure you have a
plan in place to follow up with those who attended. First, send them
a personal note, thanking them for attending and for their advice.
If they mentioned something specific that needs to be followed up
with, be sure you do follow-through. For example, they might ask for
more detailed information, an annual budget, a list of who is on your
board, or information about a specific program.

For those who seem eager to get involved, invite them to serve on
a committee of your organization—the development committee,
finance committee, marketing committee or program committee,
depending on where their interests lie. Invite them to lunch with
the executive director and/or the board chair, especially if you
think this person might be a potential board member. Add them
to your newsletter list, and invite them to events your organization
is holding. Perhaps there is a service you can provide for their
employees. For example, if you are the local affiliate of a disease-
fighting organization, you could offer to go to their place of business
to talk to their employees about the effects of blindness, lung disease,
autism, narcolepsy, etc. Notice we have not even mentioned money
to them yet! This is all part of the relationship building process. Ask
for money and you will get advice, ask for advice and eventually you
will get the money.

Here are some tools to help you plan cultivation activities and events, including a timeline, sample agenda, sample invitation letter and sample questionnaire.

**Cultivation Breakfast Plan**

Cultivation Breakfast Timeline

Week 1 Determine host.

Week 2 Meet with host to determine dates/locations, review invitation lists.

Week 4 Meet with host to determine final invitation lists/ approve letter/questionnaire.

Week 5 Prepare letters of invitation.

Week 6 Mail invitations.

Week 7 Prepare agenda/questionnaires/materials.

Week 8 Hold breakfast.

### Sample Invitation Letter

*Date*
*Name*
*Title*
*Company*
*Address*
*City, State Zip*

*Dear (NAME):*

*I would like to you to join me for a breakfast on mm/dd/yy from 7:30 a.m. to 8:45 a.m., at XYZ, address.*

*As a member of the board of directors of XYZ, I am delighted to sponsor this breakfast to introduce new friends to XYZ and the tremendously important work they are doing in our community.*

*You will be treated to a continental breakfast and a brief tour of the XYZ facility. You will also be asked to complete a short questionnaire that will help XYZ's strategic planning process. The breakfast will end by 8:45 a.m. Let me assure you that this is not a solicitation for funds.*

*Please respond by calling xxxxx at (XXX) XXX-XXXX by mm/dd/yyyy so we can plan accordingly. I know you will enjoy, along with other community leaders, hearing more about XYZ Organization and providing it with your expert advice. If you have any questions, please feel free to call me at (XXX) XXX-XXXX. I look forward to seeing you on mm/dd/yyyy.*

*Sincerely,*

*Board Member*
*Board of Directors*
*XYZ Organization*

## Sample Community Leaders' Breakfast Agenda

7:30    Breakfast

7:45    Welcome....................................................Host

7:50    An Introduction to XYZ...........................Executive Director

8:10    Questions & Answers..............................All

8:10    Completion of Questionnaire................Guests

8:20    Tour of Facility

## Sample Community Leader's Questionnaire

1. Before today, were you acquainted with XYZ? If so, what did you know about us?

_____

_____

_____

_____

_____

_____

_____

2. What community needs do you think XYZ should be serving that we currently are not addressing?

_____

_____

_____

_____

_____

_____

_____

_____

3. Are there ways we could partner with your company/organization to better serve our community?

_____

_____

_____

_____

_____

_____

_____

4. Would you be willing to become more involved with XYZ? If yes, in what capacity?

_____

_____

_____

_____

_____

_____

_____

## To Recap

♦ Successfully raising money from your business community is much like any major gift approach. It requires identification, cultivation and solicitation. One of the best ways to cultivate business donors is to first involve them and to ask for their advice before asking them for money.

♦ Cultivation activities and events can be tremendously successful in helping you make your case to the business community. These events and activities should not be used to ask for money, but to ask for advice. (The money will follow.)

◆ Cultivation can be done through one-on-one visits with business leaders or through events at which you can host a dozen or several dozen business leaders. Be sure to make it clear that you are not going to ask for money when you meet with business leaders. And be sure to follow up with guests at events.

# Chapter Seven

## Getting Started: Making the Ask

As important as relationship building is, at some point you will be ready to start asking your local business community for money. In fact, this will usually come about through the business leaders you've involved on your committees. When you are ready, remember the things we've said about raising money from businesses—do your research first, don't ask until you've formed a relationship and be prepared to make your case. If you've done all this, now you're ready to ask.

How will you ask?

It can be through your annual business appeal, matching gifts in your individual appeals, an appeal for gifts-in-kind, volunteer involvement, or a one-on-one ask.

### The Annual Business Appeal

One of the best ways I've found to approach a large number of businesses, with a small number of fundraising staff, is to run an annual business appeal involving volunteers.

Instead of appealing to businesses through the mail, establish a peer-to-peer solicitation program. First start with one or two business leaders who are already involved in your organization, either serving on a committee or on your board. Select a chair and vice chair or two co-chairs who have a passion for the mission of your organization and who have made a financial commitment to the organization from their own businesses. These two people will then help you build a team of other business leaders who can help talk to their friends and business associates. How many volunteers do you need? A good rule of thumb when soliciting people in person (which is how this appeal will take place) is to ask each volunteer to make no more than five calls. More than that and they will get frustrated, feel over-extended, and probably not even make one call.

Start small! You might have hundreds of businesses in your community, but select the ones with whom you think you will have the best chance of being successful. Select companies whose products are used by your clients, vendors, and companies who have employees that are somehow involved in or connected to your organization. For example, maybe one or more of your local banks has had teams in your golf tournament or bowl-a-thon. Or, perhaps yours is a health care facility and there are local manufacturers of medical supplies or pharmaceuticals. Ask your staff and board for a list of companies with whom they do business or where they or their spouses work. You will have a much better chance for success if the company already knows something about your organization or is one with whom you have a relationship built. This is the time to also approach those businesses who attended your advice-giving focus groups. From this list of potential donors, you should be able to identify potential volunteers. In order to determine how many volunteers you need, first make a list of all the companies in your community that you would like to ask for a contribution. Then divide that list by five and that is the number of volunteers you need.

### The Five-to-One Rule

Whenever volunteers are being asked to make a personal visit to prospective donors, they should be asked to select their five best prospects. Some enthusiastic volunteers will want to take on a list of ten, twenty or more prospects. This is a sure-fire way to guarantee that none of their calls get done. The list is just too overwhelming! If a volunteer insists on taking more than five calls, tell this volunteer to start with the "best five" prospects first, and you will "reserve" the rest of the list for the volunteer until those five calls are completed. If the volunteer does the five and comes back for more, great! But in my experience, most volunteers are ready to take a break after their five calls have been made.

practical tip

Remember that many businesses only support nonprofits with which their employees are somehow involved, so picking the right volunteers is key to the process. Research your prospective donor list; make a list of the companies you feel are likely to give if you can build a relationship with them. Divide that list into those with whom you already have identified potential volunteers and those with whom you have no current contacts. Then try to identify who in those companies you might be able to approach to volunteer for your appeal. This is where your volunteer business appeal team leaders can help. They are likely to have some connections with businesses with which you might not have a relationship. Remember, the more volunteers you have, the more companies you can approach. Once your program expands to what might seem an unmanageable size, you can divide the volunteers into teams of five people and work with team leaders. As the program expands, you might want to further refine your list into categories—financial institutions, realtors, insurance, communications and manufacturing, etc.

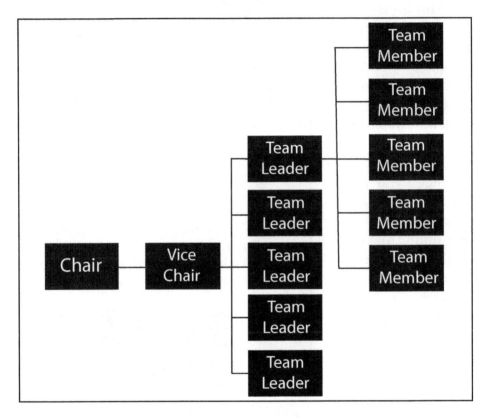

You will also need to provide the volunteers with some information about your organization that they can give to the prospective donors. But remember, these are business people, not foundation officers. They do not have the time, or perhaps the interest, to read volumes of materials. A simple one-page fact sheet can be very helpful with this group. A sample can be found in Appendix G. You can give the volunteers additional information such as brochures or annual reports to give those prospects who ask for more detailed information. A simple but professionally done annual report is a great tool that business people understand and can relate to. A list of some hints to help you prepare your annual report is in Appendix H as well.

You might want to focus your appeal on a specific project or program, such as a scholarship program for people who cannot afford your services. Your materials should clearly make a compelling case for why the local business community should support this program or project.

## The Importance of Being Prepared

Once when I worked as a development director, one of my board members called to tell me about a new corporate CEO who had just moved to town to head up one of the county's largest companies. He suggested I might try to meet with this corporate CEO to ask for a gift from his company. Knowing the importance of relationship-building, I opted for another approach instead of going straight to the "ask." Because we were in the process of recruiting volunteers to work on our annual business appeal, I decided to meet with this CEO and invite him to serve as a team leader in our campaign. When I called to schedule the appointment, he said he could give me about thirty minutes one morning later that week.

I assembled a volunteer recruitment notebook for him. In the notebook, I had our case for support, a list of our board members, a schedule for the annual corporate appeal, a fact sheet, our annual report, a list of other team leaders we had already recruited, a position description for team leaders, and some other information about our organization.

I met with him at the appointed time, and after some brief small talk, I told him I knew his time was limited (at his request, we actually talked about an hour) so I would briefly review my request and the information I had brought.

At the end of the meeting he told me he would be happy to serve as a team leader, but he said, "Before you leave, I want to tell you why I said yes to you." Of course I was 'all ears.' I wanted to know why I was successful in getting this very prominent and busy corporate leader to agree so quickly.

"I've been in town all of two weeks," he said, "and in those two weeks about fifteen nonprofits have called or come to see me, asking me for money or asking me to serve on their board, but none of them came as well prepared as you did. I know exactly what is expected of me and my company in the way of time and money. I know who else is involved and how the money we raise will help our community. I can see why you are so passionate about the organization."

One organization had a well-honed annual business appeal it had been running for a number of years. The appeal had started small. The CEO of the organization decided one year that she would ask a few business leaders, some of whom were on the board and some she knew from her community involvement, to talk to a few of their colleagues and solicit their support for the organization. The first year, she recruited four volunteers who raised about $6,000. She felt that although the appeal had been a success, there was an opportunity to raise even more money from the business community. Within a few years, the appeal grew into a hugely successful activity. The secret? Each year there was a dedicated and enthusiastic chairperson and vice chairperson. The planning started just after one year's appeal ended for the next year.

The case for support was prepared and translated into materials with which the businesses could identify and that they found easy to read. A group of team leaders was assembled representing all aspects of the business community—financial institutions, communications companies, utilities, manufacturing, real estate, etc. Each team leader recruited a team of three to five colleagues. Each team member selected prospects with which they had a relationship, either business or personal. A kickoff event for all team members was held, and team leaders attended regular report meetings. Each year this annual corporate appeal grew until, within about seven years, the organization had about 150-200 volunteers raising approximately $500,000 from the business community.

stories from the real world

He was one of our best team leaders that year; the following year he served as chair of the annual business appeal; and the following year, he was elected to our board. In the meantime, his company supported us extremely well and he helped us raise thousands and thousands of dollars.

## Training Volunteers

Your volunteers will need a training session in which they will learn how to make the "case" for your organization, and how to ask for a gift. If this is the first time these volunteers have been involved with an appeal of this type, they might need more intense training on topics such as how to schedule a meeting or how to handle objections. If your volunteers are fairly sophisticated and will be calling on their friends and peers, they might not need as much training. However, there should always be a kickoff meeting at which volunteers are given their information packets, any questions about the program are answered, and they receive training or a 'refresher' in making 'the ask.'

## Finding the Right Chair

Selection of the annual business appeal chair is a critical component in the success of the appeal. Some qualities to look for are:

- ◆ Well-known and well-respected in the business community

- ◆ Willing to devote the necessary time to the project

- ◆ Passion for the mission of the organization

- ◆ Ability to make a significant financial commitment to the appeal.

You will usually find someone with passion for your organization if you start with someone who already has some involvement or connections with your organization, perhaps someone who has had a family member or friend who has participated in your programs or have themselves participated; in other words, an 'alumnus' of your organization. If this is not possible, it could be someone who has attended your events, served on your board, or been involved with a committee or as a volunteer for your organization.

You will want to have someone who is well-known and respected in the community because others will respond better and agree to serve if they know the leader is a strong force for good in the community.

Recruit this chairperson by meeting face-to-face; this is an important decision on the chair's part and on the part of your organization. It is not to be taken lightly. As always, be prepared with everything this person will need to be effective in the job of chairperson.

Once the chair has agreed, the next step is recruiting a vice chair who the chair feels would be a good skill-set match. For example, if your chair is an enthusiastic and charismatic leader, but not so well-organized, seek a vice chair who can bring those organization skills to the team. The following year, when the well-organized person is chair, that person might seek a more dynamic speaker as vice chair.

*Keep them engaged*

Report meetings are also important so volunteers can celebrate success, provide feedback on how the program is going and receive hints from other volunteers on how to approach their prospects. Team leaders should know from the start that they will be expected to attend report meetings or send someone else from their team to report. Report meetings should be held at a convenient time, often 7 or 7:30 a.m., and should be kept to one hour at the most. At these meetings, team leaders will often share their success and help mentor newer team leaders. For many team leaders, competition is also an important part of the process and report meetings are a good time to 'brag,' encourage other teams to accept a challenge, or inspire their own teams to 'get moving' in order to catch up to the competing teams.

At the end of the appeal, plan a victory celebration. Prizes can be given to the volunteers who have raised the most money, completed the most calls, the team that has raised the highest amount, the first pledge received, and so on. Volunteers from the business community often are inspired by friendly competition. A staff or board member might want to take on the challenge of soliciting some local restaurants and other business for gift certificates that can be used as prizes.

Some ideas for token gifts that can be given to each volunteer include:

♦ A leather bookmark

♦ A coffee mug with the organization logo, filled with candy

♦ A paper weight

♦ A nice water bottle holder

Gifts that include your logo also serve as a promotional piece. You might want to give team leaders a nicer gift. The chair and vice chair should get a special gift. When I worked at a university, we gave each year's chairperson a university jacket, which became a 'badge of honor' in the business community.

The timeline for your first annual business appeal should allow for a twelve-month period. Once you have the organization structure in place, you might be able to tighten this up for future appeals.

### Business Annual Appeal Timeline

| | |
|---|---|
| Recruit Chair/Vice Chair | Month 1 |
| Develop Case for Support for Annual Appeal | Month 2 |
| Develop Preliminary Prospect List | Month 3-4 |
| Determine Number of Teams Needed<br><br>Formula:  5 calls per worker<br>             5 team members per team | Month 3-4 |

| Develop Campaign Materials | Month 3-4 |
| Recruit Team Leaders | Month 5 |
| Conduct Prospect Screening Session with Team Leaders to Finalize Prospect List | Month 6 |
| Team Leaders Recruit Teams | Month 7 |
| Assign Prospects to Teams | Month 8 |
| Conduct Kickoff Meeting | Month 9 |
| Hold First Report Meeting | Month 10 |
| Hold Second Report Meeting | Month 11 |
| Complete All Calls | Month 11 |
| Victory Celebration | Month 12 |

Developing a budget for a business appeal will depend on how many materials you will need to produce, how elaborate the materials are and how many meetings you hold. Your budget should include both anticipated income and anticipated expenses.

### Sample Budget

| *Income:* | |
| 200 businesses contacted | |
| 100 business donated @ average gift of $500 | $50,000 |
| *Expenses:* | |
| 200 Fact Sheets | $100 |
| 200 Volunteer Solicitation Packets | $300 |
| Meetings (Kickoff, Report Meetings, Victory Celebration) | $1,000 |
| Volunteer recognition gifts (40 volunteers) | $400 |
| Token gifts to donors (logo bookmarks) 100 @ $3 each | $300 |
| Consultant to help train volunteers and organize materials | $5,000 |

| Total expense: | $7,100 |
|---|---|
|  |  |
| Net Profit | $42,900 |

Following are sample position descriptions for the volunteers who will be involved in the annual business appeal and an organizational chart outlining the volunteer structure.

## Position Descriptions for Volunteers

### Business Appeal Chair

The annual business appeal committee raises money from local businesses and corporations to further the programs of XYZ Organization. Funds for this appeal are generally unrestricted and may include gifts-in-kind if they are appropriate for the organization and meet the guidelines established in the gift acceptance policies of XYZ Organization. The business appeal committee will be involved in this fundraising effort between the months of January and April each year; however, the chair position will be active for approximately nine months. The chair will be asked to serve a one-year term and will have the following responsibilities:

◆ Identify and help recruit approximately ten team leaders

◆ Assist staff with identification and evaluation of corporate and business prospects

◆ Solicit team leaders for their gifts

◆ Sign letters to be mailed to all prospects

◆ Attend and preside at kickoff meeting and report meetings

◆ Attend and preside at victory celebration

◆ Make a personal contribution to the annual appeal

◆ Secure a gift from the chair's place of business

◆ Assist in the evaluation of the appeal and plans for the following year's annual appeal

## Business Appeal Vice Chair

The annual business appeal committee raises money from local businesses and corporations to further the programs of XYZ Organization. Funds for this appeal are generally unrestricted and may include gifts-in-kind, if they are appropriate for the organization and meet the guidelines established in the gift acceptance policies of XYZ Organization. The business appeal committee will be involved in this fundraising effort between the months of January and April each year; however, the vice chair position will be active for approximately nine months. The vice chair will be asked to serve a one-year term and will have the following responsibilities:

- ◆ Identify and help recruit approximately ten team leaders

- ◆ Assist staff with identification and evaluation of corporate and business prospects

- ◆ Assist the chair with soliciting team leaders for their gifts

- ◆ Follow up with team leaders as needed during the solicitation process

- ◆ Attend and, in the absence of the chair, preside at kickoff meeting and report meetings

- ◆ In the absence of the chair, attend and preside at victory celebration

- ◆ Make a personal contribution to the annual appeal

- ◆ Secure a gift from the vice chair's place of business

- ◆ Serve as chair for the following year's annual business appeal

- ◆ Assist in the evaluation of the appeal and plans for the following year's annual appeal

## Business Appeal Team Leader

The annual business appeal committee raises money from local businesses and corporations to further the programs of XYZ Organization. Funds for this appeal are generally unrestricted and may include gifts-in-kind, if they are appropriate for the organization and meet the guidelines established in the gift acceptance policies of XYZ Organization. The business appeal committee will be involved in this fundraising effort between the months of January and April each year; however, the team leader will be active for approximately six months.

- ◆ Identify and recruit approximately five team workers

- ◆ Assist with identification and evaluation of business appeal prospects

- ◆ Solicit team members for their gifts

- ◆ Advise and encourage your team members

- ◆ Solicit approximately five businesses

- ◆ Attend and report at two to three report meetings

- ◆ Make a personal contribution to the annual appeal

- ◆ Secure a gift from the team leader's place of business

## Business Appeal Team Member

The Annual Business Appeal Committee raises money from local businesses and corporations to further the programs of XYZ Organization. Funds for this appeal are generally unrestricted and may include gifts-in-kind, if they are appropriate for the organization and meet the guidelines established in the gift acceptance policies of XYZ Organization. The business appeal committee will be involved in this fundraising effort between the months of January and April each year.

- ◆ Assist with identification and evaluation of business prospects

◆ Attend kickoff meeting

◆ Make a personal gift to the appeal

◆ Secure a gift from the team member's place of work

◆ Solicit approximately five businesses

◆ Report results to team leader in advance of report meetings

## Annual Corporate and Business Appeal Team Selection Form

Team Leader _____
Address _____
_____

Phone# _____  Fax# _____
Email _____
Companies _____
_____
_____
_____
_____

Team Member # 1 _____
Address _____
_____

Phone# _____  Fax# _____
Email _____
Companies _____
_____
_____
_____

Team Member # 2 _____
Address _____
_____

Phone# _____  Fax# _____

Email
Companies
_____
_____
_____
_____
_____
_____

Team Member # 3
Address
_____
_____
_____

Phone#                    Fax#
Email
Companies
_____
_____
_____
_____
_____

Team Member # 4
Address
_____
_____

Phone#                    Fax#
Email
Companies
_____
_____
_____
_____
_____

Team Member # 5
Address
_____
_____

Phone#        Fax#
Email
Companies
_____
_____
_____
_____
_____

Please return completed form by mm/dd/yyyy

To:

XYZ Organization
Address
Address 2
City, State Zip
Phone – Fax - Email

**Workplace Giving**

Another area in which you can raise money from your local business community is to establish a workplace giving program. You can identify these companies by first trying to find a "match" with your mission. Look for companies in your community that have a natural affiliation with your organization or cause. For example, if you serve children, there might be a company in your area that manufactures a product used by children such as crayons or toys. Or perhaps there are companies who primarily sell their services to children and families, such as fast food restaurants or candy manufacturers. You will need to be able to establish a connection with these companies and to have a strong program with a good reputation. Research the company to see if it has a history with United Way. If there is a strong connection with United Way, you might not have much chance of competing with an already existing program. If not, ask if this company would consider a workplace campaign for your organization.

If yours is a United Way agency, be sure to take advantage of the opportunity to make workplace giving presentations about your organization and suggest donor-designated gifts to your organization among employees, board members, and donors.

If your organization has community-wide appeal, you might even be able to get some of your local utility companies or department stores to include a flyer in their bills asking people to support your organization.

You might try to become a United Way agency in order to raise money through workplace giving. (This is a decision that your board needs to consider, weighing the pros and cons of becoming a United Way agency.)

When you are ready to approach these companies, ask board members, staff and other volunteers if they have an 'in' with any of these companies. There are also companies that can set up employee giving programs at companies for you. Some of these include America's Charities, Earth Share, Community Shares USA and Community Health Charities.

**Targeted Vendor Appeal**

Vendors have a natural stake in the success of your organization. Many organizations target their vendors for an annual appeal. You can start by talking with your chief financial officer and asking for a list of companies your organizations does business with. You might be surprised to find out how much money your organization puts back into the community. Some examples are insurance companies with whom your organization holds policies (this might be a significant investment on your organization's part), landscaping companies, utilities, building contractors, food service or other companies with which your organization could be spending significant dollars.

You will need clear ethical policies on how vendors are approached. It should never be done with the intent that if the vendor supports your organization they will receive special favors in the form of business contracts.

An example of a vendor solicitation policy:

### Solicitation of Donations

Only the Philanthropy Department or its designee(s) may solicit donations from vendors. Any other solicitation by members of program or administrative departments is prohibited. The

Philanthropy Department shall comply with the following general principles in soliciting donations from vendors:

◆ Any solicitation on behalf of the organization including any organizational department shall occur only by the Philanthropy Department as part of fundraising activities in the normal course (e.g., general campaign, specific drive or charitable event).

| What NOT to Do! |
| --- |
| One enthusiastic board member approached a vice president of a local bank, asking for a gift to the annual appeal. He then "threatened" that if a gift was not forthcoming, the bank would not be considered for the investment of the organization's endowment fund, which was quite substantial.<br><br>**watch out!** |

◆ Any proposal to target specific vendors for a donation (such as a request for equipment) must first be reviewed by the Legal Services and/or Corporate Compliance Department.

◆ Philanthropy Department personnel shall not link conditions of existing or potential financial relationships with the organization when soliciting donations. Philanthropy Department personnel shall avoid soliciting a vendor during a period when there is a contract negotiation in progress, if feasible.

◆ Funds received from solicitation shall be used for a charitable purpose. Funds solicited for a particular charitable purpose shall only be used for that purpose. Donations in-kind shall not be used for the benefit of particular individuals, but only for the benefit of the organization. For example, sports tickets shall be used in raffles or silent auctions to raise funds for programs, educational or other charitable activities.

## Event Sponsorship

Although event sponsorship is declining, there are still opportunities to approach corporations to sponsor your events. A few hints are to provide sponsors with good exposure, to recruit an event committee that can help solicit sponsorships, and to look for companies that will have a reason to have an affiliation with or a natural interest in the attendees at your event.

If your event audience will be an up-scale crowd, you could talk to investment firms, high-end car dealers, jewelers, or furriers, etc. to sponsor this event. If, on the other hand, your event is geared to families, you might approach more family oriented businesses, such as family restaurants, movie theaters, etc.

Businesses are often asked to contribute gifts-in-kind for events; sometimes items that will be auctioned or raffled off. Be sure to obtain the fair market value of these items from the donors so you can give them a tax receipt for the amount contributed, not the amount that the item might be sold for. And of course, remember that the people who purchase these

### Sponsoring Programs

One museum brought in a temporary exhibit of animated dinosaurs just at the height of the Jurassic Park furor. Companies were literally lining up to sponsor a dinosaur. Sponsors were invited to come in for a special preview before the exhibit opened to select their favorite dinosaur to sponsor. It became a very competitive program; the demand for Tyrannosaurus Rex, for example, was so high that the museum was able to offer alternative sponsorships for a month at a time.

practical
tip

items generally do not get a deduction because they are making a purchase, not a donation.

## Corporate Program Sponsorship

As I mentioned earlier, one form of corporate giving that is decreasing annually is sponsorship of events. Many companies are tired of events and find themselves inundated with requests to sponsor holes in a golf tournament, buy a table at a gala dinner dance, sponsor a team to run, walk, bowl, etc. They just don't want to support any more of these events.

However, corporate sponsorships of your programs can be a very meaningful way to involve people in your organization and gain their financial support.

Why not try asking companies to sponsor a scholarship for a student or someone who attends classes? Or, invite local businesses to sponsor a child, a mother or a family who is going through a program at your organization. You can be very creative! An animal rescue group, for example, could calculate how much it costs to pay for the adoption of one animal and ask local businesses to sponsor one or more animals each month. A mentoring program can figure out the cost of making a "match" between a mentor and a mentee and ask companies to sponsor a "match." A museum can determine the cost to set up a new exhibit and ask businesses to sponsor the exhibit.

Evaluate your event sponsorships and determine if sponsors are declining to sponsor events. Make a list of these sponsors and, at the same time, develop a list of programs you could invite these businesses to sponsor. Try to match up program sponsorships with companies that might have a natural connection to these programs. This could be a good opportunity for your vendors to get involved. For example, if you are looking for companies to sponsor a family involved in therapy, invite businesses that cater to families such as family restaurants, movie theaters, toy manufacturers, etc. to sponsor a family.

Some things you can invite businesses to sponsor:

- ◆ One child or family who receives services from your organization

- ◆ A lecture series on a topic of interest in your community

- ◆ Scholarships

- ◆ Animals rescued by your organization

- ◆ A "match" between a mentor and a mentee

- ◆ A meal served by your organization

- ◆ Flu shots given by your health clinic

- ◆ Faculty chairs in a school

- ◆ Field trips for students or mentees

- ◆ Concerts or performances

- ◆ Exhibits at a gallery

## Matching Gifts

Start by securing the list of matching gift companies and then try to determine if you have donors who work for these companies. You should ask for employer information whenever you are updating donor records.

You can start with your staff and board by asking if they or their spouses work for a matching gift company. Print a line on pledge cards and response envelopes, asking if the donor's employer has a matching gift program.

If you are doing a phonathon, be sure to add asking about matching gifts to the volunteer scripts or talking points.

And don't forget to mention matching gifts when soliciting major gifts.

**To Recap**

◆ An annual corporate appeal involving volunteers is a far better method than using direct mail or assigning only staff to call business leaders for their support. The appeal must be well planned and led by an enthusiastic and committed volunteer. Follow the five-to-one rule by assigning no more than five companies to each volunteer. Volunteer performance should be evaluated on an annual basis in order to determine which volunteers might need additional help, should be promoted to team leaders, or replaced.

◆ Other methods of raising money from your local business community include a targeted vendor appeal, workplace giving, and corporate sponsorship programs. You should also explore matching gift opportunities with all your donors.

# Chapter Eight

## Assuring the Future of Corporate Philanthropy—the Nonprofit Role

### IN THIS CHAPTER

···→ What changes might take place in the way businesses support the nonprofits in their communities?

···→ What changes will nonprofits need to make in order to stay competitive?

···→ What are some steps you can take now to make these changes?

One of the first steps nonprofits can take is to rethink the way they approach businesses for support, the ways they involve business leaders and the relationship-building activities they can improve upon.

In a recent survey, I found that nonprofits approached the business community in a variety of ways, some of which have been successful and others much less so.

**How Nonprofits Approach the Business Community**

In a recent survey done by CAPITAL VENTURE, participants reported using the following methods to approach businesses and corporations for financial support.

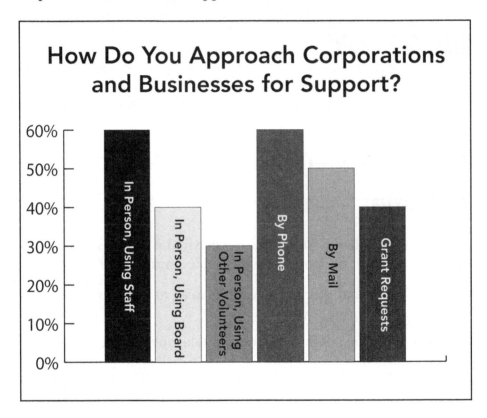

## How Do You Approach Corporations and Businesses for Support?

(Bar chart with y-axis showing 0% to 60% in 10% increments. Bars labeled: In Person, Using Staff (60%); In Person, Using Board (40%); In Person, Using Other Volunteers (30%); By Phone (60%); By Mail (50%); Grant Requests (40%).)

**Rethinking the Way You Approach Businesses**

Remember that, as with individual major gifts, businesses must be identified, cultivated and then solicited. Direct mail and casual approaches do not allow you to do the research that will make your approach more successful. Don't use the *Ready! Fire! Aim!* approach. Do your research before you approach businesses. Find out how much they give, to whom they give, who makes the decisions, how much the company is worth and how it got started. You can do research online, or talk to people who work for, do business with, or know the business's decision makers.

## Researching Your Business Community

First, know what businesses are in your community. Join your local chamber of commerce, read the *Business Journal* and the *Wall Street Journal.*

Talk to your board members and staff, your current sponsors, donors and your vendors. Ask them to help you identify companies with which they do business or have contacts.

Talk to local business leaders. Ask them to help you identify other business that could support your organization.

Read the company's website and annual report. Find out where their interests lie. Research their charitable giving programs.

Know who their top management people are and what kind of projects they are interested in. Know their financial status and how much they typically give to charities.

Remember that you can do research in a number of ways; third-party research such as electronic research, second-party research by asking other business leaders about businesses they might be familiar with, and first-hand research that includes asking the business leader themselves about their companies.

## Cultivation Activities

Plan cultivation activities and events. Invite local business leaders to see your programs in action.

One successful development officer had breakfast with a different business leader every day just to talk about ways the prospective donor might want to get involved with the organization. If this seems ambitious for you, set a goal of visiting three business leaders each month or more if you can. Set a goal you can achieve and it will pay off in the long run.

Ask your board to hold one cultivation event each month. Make sure they are inviting the people they do business with to attend these events.

### Talk the Talk

Learn to speak business-speak. Do not use jargon that might be understood by people within your agency, but not by the general public. Talk about things such as investment, ROI, bottom line outcomes (but don't use the word "outcomes," it sounds too "social service"-like and might not make sense to businesses). Use phrases such as "economic impact," "we'd like you to invest in our program," "investing in our program will improve your bottom line," and "we have low overhead and can promise you a good return on your

---

**Don't waste their time**

In his CharityChannel Press book, *Asking About Asking*, Kent Stroman offers some sage advice on how to time an "ask" meeting.

> *Here are my guidelines for managing your meeting time. Let's say the appointment was set up for 30 minutes. Budget your time as follows:*
>
> *4 minutes for introductions and pleasantries*
>
> *8 minutes (or less) to deliver the heart of your message*
>
> *8 minutes to answer the prospects' questions*
>
> *1 minute to make your 'Ask,' whatever the request is (at this point, you are 2/3 of the way into your appointment)*
>
> *5 minutes for the response/negotiation*
>
> *2 minutes to recap and schedule your next meeting*
>
> ---
>
> *28 Minutes Total (this allows you to finish ahead of time—or take 2 additional minutes to deal with any contingencies that might arise)*

practical tip

investment." Learn to read financial statements and read business books, journals and newspapers such as the *Wall Street Journal* so you know what's going on in the business world.

Adjust your timelines to meet the busy schedules of business leaders. Most business leaders like to start their day early so don't schedule meetings at 9 a.m. Try 7:30 a.m. Realize that you might have only ten or twenty minutes to "make your case," so have your meetings timed carefully in order not to waste their time.

I recall one banker with whom we were trying to arrange an appointment. Perhaps in an effort to brush us off or possibly in all sincerity, he said, "I am really busy and I don't think I can see you this week. Unless, of course," he chuckled, "you can come in when I get into my office at 6:30 a.m." Our answer: "We'll be there!" And, indeed, we showed up at this office at 6:30 the next morning, had a great meeting and enlisted his help in the campaign.

Approach business leaders with a well-prepared presentation. Do not be vague about what you are asking for; be direct! Come prepared with 'leave behind' material to cover anything you want the business leader to know or answer any question arising.

**Making Your Case**

Make sure your case has both emotional and rational reasons to give. Present your case in a way that business people will find relevant. Pie charts, easy-to-read style and community and economic impact will be important.

Develop some key communication pieces. A top notch website, an annual report, and a fact sheet are good places to start. Remember that business leaders have limited time and perhaps interest in your organization, so they will not read lengthy documents. Punch up your written materials to look professional, concise and logical.

For many companies, corporate philanthropy is seen as a way to increase their own bottom line. However, they are also looking at the bottom line of the organizations they support. Be prepared to show the business sector that you value the importance of bottom line thinking and that you have shown measurable results of the impact your organization has on the community. Start by gathering statistics on the results of your programs. For example: the decrease in the number of teen parents, an increase in graduation rates, the number of seniors who are able to stay in their homes rather than move to a health care facility, or the decrease in drug and alcohol use in the workplace. If you can show both social and economic impact on your community, businesses will be more likely to support your organization.

> *Just the facts, ma'am, just the facts!*
>
> **Sgt. Joe Friday**
> **Dragnet TV Show (circa 1950s)**
>
> **" "**

## Recruiting Volunteers to Help

Brainstorm with staff, board and development committees about who they know that could become involved in your organization's fundraising with businesses.

Expand your development committee and your board to include business leaders.

Join your chamber and attend meetings of local civic and professional organizations. These are good sources of volunteers. When you are attending these events, don't seek out familiar faces with whom to sit. Find a seat at a table where you don't know anyone. Be sure to carry plenty of business cards, and have your 'elevator speech' ready. Talk to these new potential volunteers and find out what their interests are. Not everyone is going to be interested in your organization, but the law of averages says that if you talk to enough people, you will find a number who are excited about your mission.

Be sure to have a job description for every volunteer role so you can explain to potential volunteers exactly what is expected of them. And do find out what their expectations are, too. Avoid putting a 'square peg in a round hole.'

A banker friend of mine was committed to nonprofits and involved in several community organizations, but she said that every time she was invited to serve on a board, she was automatically assigned to the finance committee. My friend was actually in the marketing department of the bank and was far more interested in serving on a marketing or development committee than she was the finance committee.

Another friend, an architect, voiced a similar dissatisfaction with nonprofits. He was invited to serve on numerous boards, and always was assigned to the facilities committee. One development officer, however, took the time to ask him about his interests. She discovered that he had a real passion for art, and wanted to serve on the collections management committee of her museum board. She was successful in recruiting him because she listened to his interests and recognized that his interests went beyond his work life.

 stories from the real world

## Approaching a Business With "The Ask"

Don't forget the LAI principle, especially the linkage component. Brainstorm with your board, staff and development committee about who they know well enough to 'make the ask.'

You need the linkage to get the appointment. Getting the appointment is 90 percent of the battle; the actual ask is easy once you get in the door. Some hints to help you get in the door:

◆ Ask a board member or volunteer who knows the prospective donor to get you an appointment.

◆ Be sure to ask for a specific time and day and show up on time.

◆ Let the scheduler know the purpose of your visit and how long it will take.

- ◆ Try calling early in the morning before the gatekeeper gets busy, or even before the gatekeeper arrives.

- ◆ Email, if possible, to schedule the appointment.

Once you get an appointment, keep it short and to the point. If the business leader wants more information, you can extend an invitation to visit your facility or meet with the expect director. Don't waste business leaders' valuable time and don't use industry jargon. Be sure to let prospective business donors know who else is involved with your organization and what other businesses are supporting you.

My challenge to you is to try at least one new method of approaching your business community and see what happens!

### To Recap

- ◆ Rethink the way you currently approach businesses if it isn't working. Try at least one new method of approaching your business community.

- ◆ Remember the LAI Principle—especially the linkage part. Getting the right volunteer or staff members to schedule the appointment is more than half the battle.

- ◆ Learn to speak business-speak. Be prepared, be concise, but be passionate.

- ◆ Involve volunteers in your business appeal. It will not only give you many more hands to share your workload, but will open doors you might have been unable to open in the past.

# Chapter Nine

## Assuring the Future of Corporate Philanthropy—the Corporate Role

### IN THIS CHAPTER

···→ What trends are emerging in the business sector that could affect your fundraising?

···→ How can you help businesses improve the company's bottom line, help your nonprofit fulfill its mission, and make a difference in their community?

···→ How can you encourage business to get their employees involved in nonprofits?

The good news is that even in times of a struggling economy many of the companies I speak to report that they are not cutting back on their funding. In fact 65 percent said that they plan to maintain or even increase giving in the coming year.

Although there was a significant decrease in corporate giving in 2009, contributions from businesses and corporations rebounded in 2010.

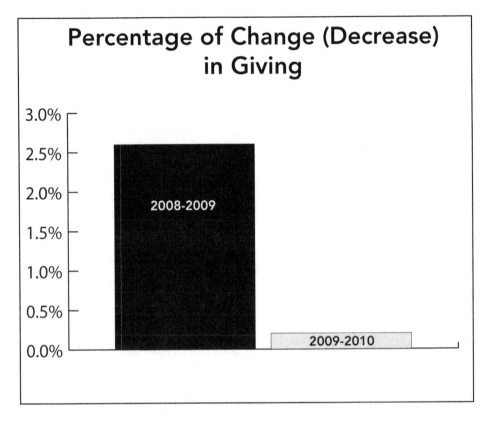

## Percentage of Change (Decrease) in Giving

2008-2009

2009-2010

More than half of surveyed corporate foundations expect to increase giving in 2011. *See chart, opposite page.*

One trend that is gaining popularity is for corporations to allow people to "vote" on sites such as Facebook for the organizations they should support. Pepsi, Chase, and AMEX are among the companies that have made this approach popular. Many fundraisers are concerned about this approach because it limits the ability for an organization to present its case to the company and build relationships with corporate leaders. Organizations that are strong in the area of social media and have built a huge following can be successful in raising a large amount of money, regardless of whether they have good programs, a strong case for support and can provide effective outcomes. Another detriment of this approach is that corporate leaders are not really involved in the decision-making and evaluation of the strength of the nonprofits who request funding.

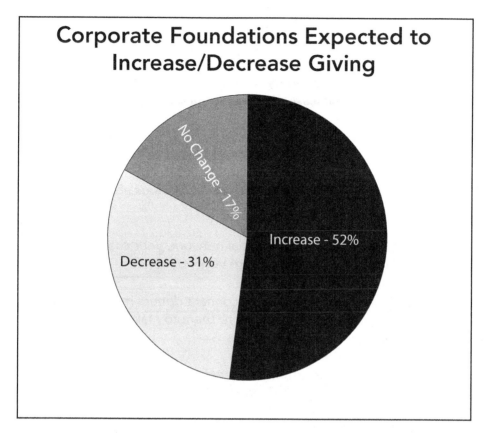

One of the major problems with this trend is that the time spent by organizations trying to get their constituents to vote for them might be better spent seeking major gifts or planning more effective fundraising strategies. And, for the companies that do not win, there is no payoff at all. If they had used these opportunities to reach out to their constituents through social media, they could direct their donors to make a donation on the organization's website rather than to "vote."

Another issue with this trend is that often donor information is compromised. Many of the company sites on which donors can vote ask for donor information which is then used by the company to market to these new "customers." In some ways, it is similar to you "selling" or trading donor information. Of course, donors have the option to not provide their contact inform, in which case they cannot "vote" for your organization.

## Social Giving Contests

*While you may be intrigued by the opportunity to raise $50,000 or more relatively painlessly through social giving promotions, be aware of the facts:*

◆ *Often the companies promoting these contests ask for your donor's personal contact information, thereby causing many of your donors to be cautious about "voting" for you.*

◆ *Unless you have a huge social network, your chances of garnering the most votes are very remote.*

◆ *You lose the opportunity to connect donors more closely to your organization and invite them to make a personal donation.*

◆ *You lose the opportunity to present your case to the company making the donation. They are simply giving to the organization that gets the most votes, not the ones that can make the best case.*

**"   "**

Before making the decision to pursue social giving contests, weigh the pros and cons carefully. You might find yourself exhausting your staff and fatiguing your donors with the constant requests of voting, instead of launching a more strategic appeal to businesses and your individual donors.

### A New Trend: B Corporations

A new trend in corporate giving is the emergence of B Corporations. Certified B Corporations are a new type of corporation that uses the power of business to solve social and environmental problems. This designation started in 2009 and, as I write this, there are almost 400 corporations who have this designation. B Corporations have been certified to be committed to positive social and environmental impact. Maryland was the first state to recognize B Corporations and many states and municipalities offer tax breaks to B Corporations, although there are currently no tax breaks offered to B Corporations from the Internal Revenue Service.

B Corporations are unlike traditional businesses because they:

◆ Meet comprehensive and transparent social and environmental standards

◆ Meet higher legal accountability standards

◆ Build business constituency for good business

What makes a B Corporation different from other corporations and why should you be aware of these differences? The main quality that distinguishes a B Corporation is that it is committed to benefitting society. These companies must, by law, be concerned with things such as quality of life and the environment.

B Corporations believe that being socially responsible makes good business sense. These businesses commit to signing a Declaration of Interdependence.

## Why is this important for you?

Identifying the B Corporations in your community can help you target businesses that are obviously committed to making the world a better place and if you can show them how your organization is changing lives, saving lives, improving the environment, etc. you will have a good chance for success with these businesses.

## Tips for Business Philanthropists

Whether you are a nonprofit professional seeking to help businesses value the process of philanthropy or a business seeking to learn more about how to support your business community, these tips can help form an interdependent community of businesses and nonprofits working together.

Nonprofit leaders should share these tips with their current business donors; it might just lead to a stronger relationship with their business community.

Invite business leaders to share these ideas with other business leaders in your community as a way for them to better understand and support the nonprofit world.

*How the business community can learn about the nonprofit community*

It is critical that businesses and nonprofits learn more about each other. We've spent a lot of time in this book talking about how nonprofits can learn more about the business community in order to build stronger relationships with business leaders before asking for money. It is equally important that business leaders learn how to give wisely. The more the business leader knows about the nonprofit sector, the easier it will be to give to the organizations that best serve the community and the customers of your business.

> One way for businesses to get to know more about the nonprofits in their community is to join AFP—the Association of Fundraising Professionals. Business leaders will get to meet the fundraisers in the community, know more about what their needs are and how they might match the interests of the business. Business leaders might be hesitant to attend a meeting filled with fundraisers, but savvy business leaders will know that this is a great place to take the pulse of the nonprofit community. Wise fundraisers will be careful not to 'pounce on' with an immediate request for a donation the brave business leader that ventures into an AFP meeting.

practical tip

Another tool available to help individuals and businesses determine the legitimacy of a nonprofit that requests funds is the state authority that regulates nonprofit fundraising activities in many states in the United States. Most states have some sort of registration requirements and those states will maintain a list of all nonprofits that are registered to do fundraising in that state. Most business leaders will do their due diligence before contributing to nonprofits, so you should make sure your organization is registered in any states in which you are required to register. This might include other states besides the one in which your organization is headquartered.

A third great tool is http://www.guidestar.org which posts all 990 forms (the required IRS form for United States charities) online so prospective donors can search the financial information and learn more about what the nonprofit does. There are also 'watchdog' groups such as the Better Business Bureau that monitor nonprofit activities. Business leaders might rely on these sources for information. Be sure your Form 990 is accurate and effective.

*Invite business leaders to get involved*

Most nonprofits are more than eager to involve local business leaders, and many executives and mid-level managers find this work is not only rewarding, but a change of pace from their daily routine. Often they learn new skills as a result of their nonprofit involvement. I know one executive who welcomed being invited by a local nonprofit to participate in its

> One of the best ways for business leaders to understand how the nonprofit world works is to get directly involved in it. Encourage business leaders to volunteer for your nonprofit before you ask them to make a donation. Encourage them to invite employees to get involved and have them report back on their experiences. Many businesses have policies that they only contribute to organizations in which their employees are involved.

practical tip

strategic planning process because it helped her learn more about the planning process, which helped her do her job better. Be sure to show business leaders how involvement with the nonprofit community can help their staff members be better employees.

If you make it easy for business leaders to get involved in your organization, it will pay off for you in many ways. Your organization will be the beneficiary of time and talent the business leaders can offer as board members and volunteers and you will be more likely to raise money from these businesses if their leaders are involved with your organization.

*Make it fun, easy and rewarding for business Leaders to serve on your board*

Here are some hints to make it easy to recruit business people for your board:

◆ Hold your meetings at a convenient time for business leaders (often early morning is good, or right after work).

◆ Keep meetings brief and stick to the agenda (usually 90 minutes is sufficient time to discuss necessary business).

◆ Have a "mission moment" at each board meeting in which board members get to hear form a client, a staff member or someone who has benefitted from your programs. Make the stories compelling.

◆ Send out all reports in advance to eliminate wasting time reading reports during the meeting.

◆ Let committee chairs establish the best time for their committee to meet, and provide a staff person to take notes and prepare reports for committees.

◆ Balance your board with an adequate amount of business people so the newcomer to the board doesn't feel like the "lone wolf" by being the only business person on the board.

◆ Start meetings on time, end on time, and follow *Robert's Rules of Order.*

◆ Make sure your boardroom looks professional, is neat and clean, has enough seats, and provides all necessary equipment such as LCD projectors and laptops, along with a phone conference system for board members who might be unable to attend in person.

◆ Provide board members with a board manual with pertinent data but don't expect them to read through extraneous material. (I once sat on a board that provided each board members with a 5″ binder containing, among other things, the complete personnel manual.)

◆ Provide education for the board but keep it exciting and limit "training" to areas board members really need to know.

Another way you can help local businesses is to offer them advice on how they can become more philanthropic. The following ideas might help them start or increase their philanthropic giving. Sometimes businesses want to help their communities, but they are just not sure how to do it.

## Hints to help businesses establish criteria for giving

The sad reality for business leaders is that you can't support every worthy cause in your community. Determine what type of organizations your company wants to support and what type of giving you will do. Here are some questions for business leaders to ask:

*Is your company interested in the arts, in health care, or in education? Are there constituents of the organization that are also customers or potential customers for your company? Do you want to support capital projects that often offer more recognition, but also involve multi-year commitment? Would your company be more interested in supporting programs directly? Do you want to sponsor events which, such as capital projects, offer good exposure for your company, but often have high overhead expenses so might not directly benefit the people in the community who need help?*

You need to think about the impact on your business if you offer employees a day on the golf course, fill a table at a black tie event, or sponsor a team to run, bowl, walk, dance, etc. Although these events offer the opportunity for your employees to mix and mingle, and market your business, they also might take valuable time away from the office when you could be short-staffed and could create negative feelings for those employees not participating in these events.

*Establish a philanthropy budget*

You can't give it all away. I've made it a point to drive home to the nonprofit fundraisers the fact that businesses are in business to make money for their stockholders or owners, not to give it away. Being a good corporate citizen means that you will want to contribute to organizations that truly make a difference, and in every community there are dozens or even hundreds of these groups. Your company's giving will be easier to manage if you establish a budget for philanthropy during your regular budget cycle. Many nonprofits will contact you during your budgeting cycle so that they can be included. Or they might contact you early in the year before your budget is allocated to other needs. Let nonprofits know your budgeting cycle and when they should approach you to be considered in your charitable budget.

Determine the ways you will support nonprofits: marketing dollars, philanthropic dollars, matching gifts, etc.

Most businesses have a larger marketing budget than they have set aside for philanthropic giving. Supporting your local nonprofit community can be a fantastic marketing tool and one that really helps create a win-win situation. You might have a marketing budget that can cover some things such as event sponsorships which many businesses view as more of a marketing investment than a true philanthropic contribution. From the business standpoint, the tax consequences usually are similar so you might consider having a philanthropy budget and a marketing budget for sponsorships.

Another option is to match gifts made by your employees. This not only assures that your company is supporting projects and organizations that are important to your employees, but it encourages individual philanthropy on their part as well. The Council for the Advancement and Support of Education (CASE) is a great source of information on matching gifts programs.

*Involve your employees*

Many companies appoint an employee charitable giving committee. This encourages your employees to be involved in their community and gives them a feeling of empowerment within the company. You can appoint employees from all divisions, not just management, to serve on this committee. You will get different viewpoints and give employees the satisfaction that knowing their opinions are important.

You might also involve employees in volunteer activities and have them learn more about the nonprofits in your community. This can also teach them valuable skills that will help them in their jobs. Many businesses invest in their employees by sending them to leadership programs that help prepare them for board service.

*Hold the nonprofit community accountable*

Once you've made a contribution to a nonprofit, you have every right to hold it accountable for the money you've given. Foundations often have extensive reporting requirements. You might not need to go into a formal reporting process, but the organization should, at the very least, thank you for your gift, let you know how the money was used and provide you with appropriate acknowledgment and recognition.

If you have any doubts that the organization is not using your money judiciously, ask for their 990 form or search for it on http://www.guidestar.org.

*Define a win-win situation*

Determine what your company is looking for in the way of payback. Are you looking for public recognition, increased sales, awareness of the community, the satisfaction that comes from being a good corporate citizen? Do you want increased opportunities for your employees to be involved or direct advantages for your employees?

Seek out the organizations that provide you with the things you are looking for, resulting in a true win-win situation.

## Seeking Help to Develop a Corporate Giving Program

There are companies that can help businesses develop a corporate giving program. Most of these are managed by people who have spent time in the nonprofit sector and are now focusing their efforts on helping create win-win partnerships among businesses and nonprofits. In the Appendix K you will find a guide developed by Peter Parker of NPCatalyst that might prove helpful for businesses that want to expand their community giving efforts.

So, is corporate philanthropy worth the effort? I say a resounding, "yes!" It benefits the nonprofit community, the business and makes the community a better place in which to live and work. And who isn't interested in that?

However, all of this does not happen without a lot of cooperation between the nonprofit sector and the business community. Employees of businesses and nonprofits need to better understand each other. Boards need to be strengthened by having people with business acumen serve. Each sector needs to learn more about each other.

I hope this book will serve as a beginning step to building stronger communities through the mutual work of the business and nonprofit sectors. And that together we can raise the level of corporate giving in the future.

## To Recap

- ◆ Businesses can do so much to benefit the local nonprofit community, not only by investing their dollars, but by giving of their employee time, their expertise and their passion for the community.

- ◆ Businesses should be wise givers and should do their due diligence before contributing to every nonprofit with their hand out.

- ◆ There are many ways businesses can support their local community. Gifts-in-kind, matching gifts, corporate grants, cash gifts, volunteer time and expertise are all important.

- ◆ Together, the business and nonprofit sectors, can not only increase the level of corporate philanthropy, but improve and transform their communities into better places to work and live.

# Appendix A—Glossary

**990 Form:** An Internal Revenue Service form that public charities must file each year to prove compliance with tax laws.

**Annual fund:** Fundraising campaign, conducted each year, to provide financial resources to conduct annual operations.

**Articles of Incorporation:** The official document that establishes a corporation, as stipulated by the laws of a particular state.

**Ask, the:** The request for a contribution or pledge. Most effective ask is when adequate research has been conducted on the prospect and a specific amount is presented for the prospect to consider.

**Audit:** The process completed by an auditor, involving analysis, tests, and confirmations that result in an issued opinion on whether year-end financial statements reflect the actual financial activity and condition of the organization for the time period in question.

**B Corporation:** "Benefit Corporation" is organized with the intent that the company will be socially responsible. Some states or municipalities offer tax benefits to B Corporations.

**Balance sheet:** The statement of financial position.

**Budget:** The organization's plan of action expressed in dollars (income and expense); allows the organization to track actual performance against a board-approved plan.

**Capital campaign:** A substantial fundraising effort intended to provide for major organizational needs, such as buildings, endowments or other major expenses.

**Case statement:** A document that explains the what, why and how of a fundraising campaign.

**Cash flow:** The amount and timing of money that moves into and out of an organization.

**Certified Public Accountant (CPA):** An accountant who has satisfied the statutory and administrative requirements of the state in which the accountant is to be licensed.

**Cause-related marketing:** The public association of a for-profit company with a nonprofit organization intended to promote the company's product or service and to raise money for the nonprofit.

**Consolidated financial statement:** A report that combines the assets, liabilities, revenues, and expenses of a parent organization and any subsidiary organizations.

**Contribution:** A gift or donation given to an organization for which the donor receives no direct private benefits in return.

**Corporation:** A corporation is a formal business association with a publicly registered charter recognizing it as a separate legal entity having its own privileges, and liabilities distinct from those of its members. There are many different forms of corporations, most of which are used to conduct business.

**Corporate foundation:** A private foundation established by a company to direct its charitable giving. Usually has a board composed of corporate officials and makes grants in fields related to corporate activities and/or in communities where the corporation operates.

**Diversification:** Having a variety of funding types and sources so that the nonprofit organization is not unduly dependent on a handful of sources.

**Donation:** A gift to a charity or worthwhile cause.

**Donor:** An individual or organization that makes a pledge, grant or contribution to the nonprofit.

**Earned revenue:** Income an organization obtains through exchange transactions such as fees; ticket sales; and certain, but not all, government contracts.

**Employee benefits:** Non-cash employee compensation such as health insurance and retirement plans. These benefits are voluntarily or contractually supplied by an employer, as compared to payroll taxes; accounted for as personnel costs.

**Endowment:** A fund with its donated assets permanently restricted by the donor. Interest or income generated may be unrestricted, temporarily restricted, or permanently restricted.

**Entity:** A person, corporation, government, or other organization.

**Entrepreneur: A** person who organizes and manages any enterprise, especially a business, usually with considerable initiative and risk.

**Fair market value:** Amount for which an investment could be sold between willing parties (i.e., not a forced or liquidation sale). Method used to determine its value at the time of donation to a nonprofit.

**Fiscal year:** A twelve-month period selected by an organization for reporting purposes. A nonprofit cannot change its fiscal year without informing the IRS.

**Foundation:** A not for profit organization which is set up by individual, family, community or business for the purpose of distributing charitable gifts.

**Full-time equivalent (FTE):** The number of positions at an organization that equal full-time employment. For example, two full-time and two half-time staff people equal a total of four employees, but three FTE.

**General operating support:** Funds for running an organization which are not restricted to any program.

**Generally accepted accounting principles (GAAP):** The rules for financial reporting that ensure that financial reports are relevant, reliable, consistent, and presented in a way that allows the reader to compare the results to prior years and to other organizations.

**Governance or board development committee:** A committee formed by the board and usually consisting of board members plus the executive director, existing to assist the board to govern well, through making recommendations about how the board should operate, and leading board development activities on behalf of the board.

**Grant:** Generally a cash award from an organizational funder [the grantor](foundation, corporation, or government agency)to a grant-eligible organization (nonprofit or government) [the grantee] in order to accomplish a specific purpose, such as starting a project, serving the needy, or purchasing a piece of equipment, etc. Grants are often funded in response to a proposal from the grantee, although some are awarded through requests for proposals (RFPs). Government contributions are grants when their purpose is to provide a service for public benefit, rather than to serve the direct and immediate needs of the grantor.

**Grantee:** The recipient of a grant; also known as the grant recipient or beneficiary.

**Grant monitoring:** Continuing evaluation of the progress of the programs funded by a donor in order to determine if the terms and conditions of the grant are being met and if the objectives of the grant are being achieved.

**In-kind donation:** Services or goods contributed without charge. A contribution of equipment, supplies, services or other tangible resource to be used by the charity, as distinguished from monetary contribution; some organizations also might donate the use of space or staff time as an in-kind contribution.

**LLC:** An abbreviation that refers to a Limited Liability Company, a flexible form of business enterprise that blends elements of partnership and corporate structures organizations.

**Letter of Intent:** Signed, written document which details the level of gift, payment schedule, intentions, conditions, naming preferences, etc. of the donor. A *letter of intent* is a document outlining an agreement between two or more parties before the agreement is finalized.

**Leverage:** Using assets or borrowing against its value to obtain or control greater amounts of money. A method of grant making designed to attract additional funding. Leverage occurs when an amount of money is given with the express purpose of attracting larger funding from other sources or of providing the organization with the tools it needs to raise other kinds of funds; sometimes known as the 'multiplier effect.'

**Major gifts:** Individual, corporate or foundation pledges and contributions of an amount less than the leadership gifts category that are paid off within agreed upon timeline. (Amount of gift varies from organization to organization based upon giving history and size of campaign goal.)

**Marketing:** The process or technique of promoting, selling, and distributing your product/service/brand.

**Matching gifts:** Gifts made by an employer to match gifts made by employees to qualified charitable organizations.

**Mission Statement:** A mission statement reflects an organization's core values and reason(s) for existing. It should capture what an organization does, why it does it, how it does it and for whom it does it. A mission statement broadly addresses the current and future purpose(s) of the organization.

**Naming/Dedicatory Opportunity:** Those physical buildings, rooms, structures, endowments, programs, etc. which have been assigned a dollar value which can be identified with donors who contribute an amount equal to the designation. In addition to overall recognition, those who contribute for specific naming opportunities might have a plaque or other forms of recognition adjacent to their selection indicating the name of the donor and/or if it is a memorial or gift in honor of an individual, family or group.

**Net assets:** The resources ultimately available to the organization after paying all liabilities. (Assets – Liabilities = Net Assets). Found on the Statement of Financial Position.

**Nonprofit organization:** An entity that possesses the following characteristics: 1) Receives significant resources from donors who do not expect equivalent value in return, 2) Operates for purposes other than to provide goods or services at a profit, and 3) Lacks an identifiable individual or group of individuals who holds a legally enforceable residual claim. Being nonprofit does not automatically confer tax exemption.

**Opportunity cost:** The income that could be obtained if the resources committed to one action were used in the most desirable alternative action.

**Overhead activity:** The combination of administrative and fundraising activities.

**Partnership:** A form of business where two or more parties are responsible for the debts of the company and divide the income according to a predetermined arrangement.

**Pledge:** An amount that the donor agrees to contribute over a period of time or by a certain date.

**Profit:** The money an organization earned or took in after paying all associated expenses. Nonprofit organizations can make the equivalent of a profit, but those funds cannot go to any individuals; they must remain within the organization to be used for its charitable purpose.

**Prospect:** An individual, foundation, or corporation who is identified as having capacity and assigned for a solicitation.

**Quasi-endowment:** A fund established by a governing board which sets aside unrestricted funds "as if" they were an endowment with the intent never to spend them. These monies must be reported as unrestricted funds since the board could lift the conditions at any time.

**Rating:** The dollar amount that is determined by the solicitor, leadership, and staff to be presented to the prospect for their consideration.

**Real property:** Land (including land improvements) buildings, and structures, but excluding movable machinery and equipment.

**Receipt:** An official requirement for charities to acknowledge, with the amount, all gifts over $250 from any donor within the calendar year. Most charities provide a written acknowledgment for all gifts

**Restricted Funds:** Monies that are donor designated to be used for a specific purpose or in a specific way by the recipient

**Revenues:** Strictly speaking, earned income rather than donations, however, many nonprofits include all income as revenue.

**ROI:** *Return on Investment:* ROI is one of several commonly used approaches for evaluating the financial consequences of business investments, decisions, or actions; the value of effort when taking into account the time and cost of planning and producing the activity.

**S Corporation:** A United States corporation in which the company's income and/or loss is passed to its shareholders. Shareholders report this business income or loss on their personal tax returns.

**Sole Proprietorship:** A business owned and operated by one person who is solely liable for its obligations and receives all of the profits.

**Solicitation:** The process (meeting) which takes place between the solicitor and the prospect at which time the request for support is made.

**Solicitor:** The person who is assigned to ask someone to support the campaign.

**Stakeholder:** Anyone that has an interest in an organization's work, i.e. leaders, staff, donors, volunteers, recipients of services, etc.

**Strategic plan:** A formal document summarizing board decisions about the how the organization will help achieve desired outcomes over the next few years.

**Suspect:** An individual, foundation, or corporation who is identified as having capacity, but might not be qualified yet to be cultivated or solicited.

**S.W.O.T.:** Strengths, Weaknesses, Opportunities, Threats. Analysis conducted as part of the planning process.

**Taxpayer Identification Number (TIN):** The number used to identify an employee (SSN) or employer (EIN) for tax reporting purposes.

**Tax exempt:** Not required to pay specific taxes, generally in return for some public benefit. Organizations that are tax-exempt under IRC 501(c)(3) are eligible to receive foundation, corporate or individual donations.

**Tax Exemption:** IRS provides tax deductions for valid gifts to certain nonprofit organizations. Donors may not take deductions for gifts where they receive a benefit from the charity. For example, monies paid for a cruise or paid for a purchase at a charity auction would not be deductible even if the check for the cruise were made out to the charity. Monies paid "over" the fair market value are deductible.

**Third Sector:** Another term for the nonprofit industry.

**Unrelated business income:** Income from business activities that do not promote or advance a nonprofit's charitable or exempt purpose. This income is taxable and must be reported to the IRS on Form 990-T. UBIT is the term used for unrelated business income tax.

**Venture Philanthropy:** Concept through which enterprising donors provide money, time and talent to nonprofits, often for cutting-edge programming, and usually with heavy involvement of the donors. Venture philanthropists are often younger, involved in hi-tech industries and are considered entrepreneurs.

**Vision:** A shared image of what impact you envision in the future.

# Appendix B—CRO's Top 100 Socially Responsible Corporations

*Corporate Responsibility Magazine,* or simply *CR Magazine,* is devoted to identifying and making public the top socially responsible corporations. Its 100 Best Corporate Citizens List publishes the top 100 socially responsible corporations on an annual basis, determined after thorough research by the *CR* staff members who review news stories, court cases and other public information. The *CR* organization gives companies red cards and yellow cards if they do not meet the criteria for being socially responsible.

The *CR* organization uses criteria from the Global Reporting Initiative, the Carbon Disclosure Project, and the UN Global Compact. It also seeks input from investors and nonprofits.

It issues an overall "Top 100" but also lists the best companies in specific industries.

To learn more about *Corporate Responsibility Magazine* and the Top 100 list, visit http://www.thecro.com.

# Appendix C—Sample Gift Acceptance Policies

Sample Gift Acceptance Policies

I.    General Policies and Guidelines

    A.    The foundation and university through the campaign, welcomes expressions of interest and financial support, regardless of size or form, from any alumnus, parent, friend, corporation, foundation or similar source.

            The campaign volunteers and appropriate officers and staff from the foundation and university are available and would be pleased to meet with any prospective donor, without obligation, to discuss areas of interest, the university's needs or objectives, types of commitments, options for payment, estate planning, the tax consequences of a possible commitment, and otherwise to provide every possible appropriate assistance to a prospective donor.

    B.    Commitments to the campaign may take the form of one or a combination of the following:  cash, pledges, appreciated securities or other personal assets, gifts-in-kind, deferred or planned gifts including charitable remainder trusts, charitable gift annuities, matured bequests, insurance policies, a gift of a residence with or without a retained life interest, and, under special circumstances, will commitments. (See section II.)

C.  All philanthropic commitments made to the foundation or university beginning July 1, 1993 through June 30, 1998, and/or selected commitments made during the previous twelve months (July-June) and approved by the Campaign Steering Committee will be credited toward the campaign goal.

All gifts to the annual fund, President's Club, Rocket Club and other philanthropic support arriving from outside the campaign structure during the campaign period will be credited toward the ongoing support component of the goal.

D.  The university's board of trustees, the leadership of the campaign and appropriate university and foundation officers reserve the right to accept or (in cases where absolutely necessary) decline any financial commitment, which is offered. They also reserve the right to determine how any commitment will be credited or how such a commitment will be recognized.

Commitments will be publicly recognized consistent with the guidelines published in the campaign literature and commemorative opportunities brochure.

Published guidelines regarding the minimum funding levels for "named" commemorative opportunities are subject to exception under mitigating circumstances upon the recommendation/approval of the campaign's leadership and appropriate foundation and university officials. In general, all commitments will be credited in campaign attainment totals at no less than the amount projected to be acceptable for federal income tax deduction.

E.  All potential or proffered commitments will be individually reviewed. Commitments of unusual size, designation, form and/or schedule of payment will be carefully evaluated. A prospective donor is encouraged to request and might expect a written position from the campaign's leadership and/or Foundation and University representatives regarding a potential commitment prior to making such a commitment.

F.  Although representatives of the campaign and University will provide all appropriate assistance (please see paragraph 2, item A, Section I), the ultimate responsibility regarding evaluations, tax deductibility and/or similar local, state and/or federal legal compliance issues regarding commitments rests with the donor.

G.  The university, through the campaign's leadership, other volunteers, or representatives of the foundation and university will neither knowingly seek nor accept any commitment regardless of size, tender, designation or other parameter which it believes is not in the potential donor's best interest to give.

In the event that such a commitment is accepted and the circumstances brought to the attention of the campaign's leadership, such a commitment will not be considered binding on the part of the donor, and any transfer of assets made in conjunction with the commitment will be returned or repaid.

Furthermore, a donor may upon written request seek, without explanation, to withdraw his or her commitment. Return of payments may be made under extremely mitigating circumstances and where allowable by law. In some cases, it might not be possible to return payments, which have been committed to specific projects.

H.  All volunteers and representatives of the foundation and university are committed and responsible to not seek, encourage nor accept any commitment that is potentially not in the university's best interest and/or which is inconsistent with the fiduciary and/or moral responsibilities commensurate with their campaign or university roles.

Potential commitments, which could be modified or refused, could evolve around one or a combination of the following:

1.  A desire to develop or otherwise fund a program which would seem to be inconsistent with the university's traditional, current, or future educational mission as determined by the University's administration.

2.  A desire to develop a particular program of interest to the university, but for which the donor is unwilling or unable to commit the resources necessary either to see the project through to completion or to maintain in perpetuity a project which would not be self-sustaining.

3.  A desire to designate or restrict a commitment in a way which is inconsistent with policies or local, state or federal statutes regarding race, creed, national origin, religion or a similar issue.

I.  While all commitments regardless of size and designation are welcomed, commitments of immediate cash, negotiable assets, or short-term pledges are the form of donor commitments, which have the greatest immediate impact on the university's needs.

This is not meant to disparage or in any way to discourage other types of commitments which do not include "immediate cash."

The rationale and urgency of university-wide programs create immediate and short-term funding needs. Furthermore, a primary consideration in any prospective donor's decision to support the objectives of the campaign is to ensure, in the most immediate and expedient way possible, the brightest future for

University.

J.   No commitment will be credited against the campaign goal without adequate written documentation of the commitment from the donor. Such documentation may be in the form of a pledge card, letter of intent, personal letter or similar document. Exceptions to the preceding require the approval of the university president, campaign chair and campaign director.

K.   Preliminary decisions regarding the reporting of commitments to the campaign will be made by the campaign director and the university president using appropriate campaign policies and guidelines data accompanying the commitment, comments from the solicitor and campaign precedence of a similar nature.

These decisions (appropriately documented in the campaign's permanent files) will be reflected individually and collectively within the monthly campaign attainment report, letters of acknowledgment and similar documentation. Monthly attainment reports will be submitted to the university president for approval prior to distribution. If necessary, the crediting, etc., of controversial commitments will be referred to the campaign steering committee for decision.

All preliminary or final decisions regarding the evaluation and/or crediting (amount, source, etc.) of commitments to the campaign are subject to review and adjustment with the written approval of the campaign chair and campaign director upon receipt of new information, a request for change by the donor, an additional commitment by the donor, and/or other mitigating circumstances.

L.   During the period of the campaign all alumni, parents and other friends will be asked to maintain or increase their support of the on-going annual fund program in addition to making commitments in support of the campaign.

II.     Standards for Reporting Certain Types of Gifts and Pledges

A.     Donors are encouraged to fulfill pledge commitments within five, but preferably, three years. Exceptions will be considered upon request.

B.     *Cash:* Cash gifts will be reported at full value as of the date received by the University.

C.     *Securities:* Securities will be counted at the average of the high and low market value on the date the donor relinquished control of the assets in favor of the Foundation. Closely held stock may be valued at the per share cash purchase price of the most recent transaction. Normally, this will be the buy-back transaction of the donor. If no buy-back is consummated during the campaign, the stock cannot be credited to the campaign.

D.  Gifts of Property

1. *Gifts-in-Kind:* Gifts-in-kind (e.g., equipment, books, software and the like that can be put to immediate use) for which donors qualify for a charitable gift deduction under current IRS rules should be counted at their full market value.

2. *Real and Personal Property:* Gifts of real and personal property (e.g., land, houses, jewelry, paintings, antiques, rare books, etc.) exceeding $5,000 in value should be reported at the fair market value placed on them by an independent, expert appraiser at the time the donor relinquishes control in favor of the Foundation.  Gifts of $5,000 and under may be

reported at the value declared by the donor or a
qualified on-campus expert.

E.  *Charitable Remainder Trusts and Gift Annuities:* Gifts made
to establish charitable remainder trusts and gift annuities
should be credited at fair market value of the assets given.

F.  *Charitable Lead Trusts:* Only the income received from
a charitable lead trust during a pledge payment period,
not to exceed five years or the duration of the campaign
(whichever is longer), will be reported.

G.    *Trusts Administered by Others:* Only the fair market value
of assets placed in trust during the period of the campaign,
to which the institution has an irrevocable right to all
or a predetermined portion of the trust income, will be
reported.

H.  *Non-government Grants and Contracts:* Grant income
from private, non-government sources will be reported;
contract revenue will be excluded.  The difference between
a private grant and contract should be judged on the
basis of the intentions of the awarding agency and the
legal obligation incurred by the university in accepting the
award. A grant, such as a gift, is bestowed voluntarily and
without expectation of any tangible compensation; it is
donative in nature. A contract carries an explicit quid pro
quo relationship between the source and the university.

I.  *Testamentary pledge commitments:* Testamentary pledge
commitments or will commitments from testators, who are
at least seventy years old, will be credited to the campaign
total at the value established in writing by the testator
unless there are mitigating circumstances and/or such a
decision would conflict with other campaign policies or
guidelines.

Will commitments, where the testator does not indicate
a specific amount to university (a residual provision) or

where the testator does not wish to be "credited" with a specific amount, will be credited at a minimum value level of $1,000.

Commitments in this category will be recognized consistent with the general guidelines regarding same except in cases where such a designation will necessitate the short-term commitment of university or foundation funds not currently budgeted to support the area designated by the potential donor.

J.  *Life Insurance:* Fully paid up or otherwise vested insurance policies which are assigned to the foundation will be credited at the full face or cash surrender value of the policy, whichever is greater. As such, commitments will be recognized as outlined in the campaign brochure and the commemorative opportunities brochure unless the donor requests other special arrangements.

Donors of such commitments may designate their gifts in any way consistent with foundation or campaign guidelines previously outlined, subject, of course, to the ultimate approval of the campaign's leadership.

Commitments of insurance where ownership is assigned to the Foundation but where the policy is not yet paid up will be credited to the campaign at the current cash value of the policy or the value of the paid up premiums whichever is greater. Subsequent payments of premiums by the donor will be added to the value assigned to this commitment.

Commitments in this category, which do not mature during the campaign period, qualify for commemorative opportunities and recognition at a level consistent with the value of the policy as it was credited to the campaign, i.e., cash value plus on-going premium payments.

Exceptions to the preceding may be made by campaign leadership and foundation representatives in such cases where the commitment is made by an individual of seventy years of age or older and/or where other mitigating circumstances exist.

In the event that the donor discontinues premium payments, the donor's gift record, campaign attainment figure and similar records will reflect the value of the policy as of that date and/or as received by the foundation.

K. *Bequests:* Bequests (matured will commitments) will be credited at the value established at the time of probate. Bequests of real estate or other tangible personal property (e.g., paintings. antiques, jewelry) will be credited at the appraised value of the property at the time it is transferred, provided there is no unacceptable restriction on its liquidation.

L. *Restrictions:* Given the objective of the campaign and the relatively short-term cash needed to meet campaign needs, the following types and/or levels of commitment are not encouraged:

   1. Will commitments by donors less than seventy years of age, unless there are mitigating circumstances and/or potential commitment is part of a long-range philanthropic commitment to University including annual giving and a commitment of capital other than that represented by the proposed will commitment.

   2. The creation of a charitable gift annuity where the potential donor has not reached 60 years of age and/or where there is an intervening beneficiary.

   3. Commitments of unpaid insurance policies under $25,000 where the potential donor has not reached sixty years of age.

Under no circumstances does the campaign's leadership want to encourage a situation whereby a donor converts an existing pattern of unrestricted cash gifts to the annual fund into an annual fixed payment of an insurance premium.

Under any of the circumstances outlined in the preceding points, numbers 1, 2 and 3 are what appear to be similar situations volunteers are strongly encouraged to seek instead of the proposed commitment, an increased annual fund commitment and a pledge to the campaign.

This alternative is desirable in almost all cases, even if the potential value of the proposed will commitment, insurance policy, etc., is greater than the potential alternative annual fund and/or campaign pledge.

The preceding is viable up to the point where the potential donor may refuse to make any commitment. An exception to guideline "I" might exist where the potential donor has substantial resources but is reluctant to commit assets except on an experimental or incremental basis.

Request for exceptions to guideline A. 1 must be made in writing to the campaign director and/or campaign steering committee.

# Appendix D—Sample Corporate Guidelines for Reviewing Funding Requests

1. Amount requested.

2. Purpose, history and current activities of organization.

3. Purpose/objective of primary programs.

4. Segment of the community these programs will benefit/serve.

5. Demographic profile of the community served including statistics on low- and moderate-income and any military population served.

6. How the objectives of the programs will be achieved and the timeframe.

7. Method of evaluation of program's success.

8. Plans for the future.

9. Current budget including sources of income.

10. Total funding needed and projected sources.

11. Most recent audited financial report and most recent unaudited profit and loss statement.

12. Other corporate and foundation support (name and amount) from previous twelve-month period.

13. Proof of IRS tax-exempt status; and

14. List of key management and board of directors.

# Appendix E—Corporate Prospect Screening Form

RATING of COMPANY's ABILITY:

A. $100,000 +

B. 50,000 +

C. 25,000 +

D. 10,000+

E. 1,000 +

LINKAGES WITH COMPANY/ MANAGEMENT

I. Current or past donor to our organization

II. Vendor

III. Management or employees volunteer with organization

INTEREST CODES:

1. Active interest in organization.
2. Limited Interest in organization.
3. No interest in organization.

Screener: _____

| Company Name & Contact Person | Rating | Interest | Linkage | Suggested Solicitor | Other Pertinent Information |
|---|---|---|---|---|---|
| | | | | | |
| | | | | | |
| | | | | | |
| | | | | | |
| | | | | | |

# Appendix F—Questionnaire/Checklist for Case Statement Evaluation

Look for the feedback in the following area:

- ❏ Does it elicit emotional as well as rational "reasons" to give?
- ❏ Does it tell your potential donors how their gift will make a difference?
- ❏ Does it evoke a sense of the history and long-term importance of your organization and its work?
- ❏ Does it offer proof that your plan will work?
- ❏ Are the benefits to the donor clearly stated?
- ❏ If you include graphs or charts, are they striking?
- ❏ Is it concise?
- ❏ Is it reader oriented rather than organization oriented?
- ❏ Does it emphasize "opportunity" for the donor rather than "need" of the organization?
- ❏ Is the information presented in a logical order?
- ❏ Is it readable with short sentences and paragraphs?
- ❏ Is the typeface appropriate to your organization's appeal?
- ❏ Is there enough blank space to make it easy to read?

❑ Is the type large enough for reading by older prospects?

❑ Is the cover "striking?"

❑ Is the paper stock attractive without looking expensive?

❑ If you use photographs, are they effective and cropped to maximize their impact? (Photos should not include more than two or three people. Large group shots lose dramatic impact.)

# Appendix G—Sample Fact Sheet

---

**Museum Name**
**Museum Logo**

400 ABC Avenue                                      Museum 111-222-3333
Anytown, ST 10000-1001                        Planetarium 444-555-6666
Hours 9 a.m. to 5 p.m. Tuesday – Saturday
1:30 p.m. to 5 p.m. Sunday

Accredited by American Association of Museums (AAM)

**Museum Staff:**

John Doe, Museum Director

Jane Doe, Planetarium Director

James J. James, Curator

Sally Jones, Education Director

Joe Jones, Development Director

Susie Queue, Volunteer Coordinator

John Q. Public, Collections and Exhibits Manager

**Museum Programs:**

- Outreach programs provided to classrooms in Lancaster County.
- Field trips to the museum, including tours by trained Docents, visits to Discovery Room, Herpatarium, Planetarium.
- Educational Discovery Kits for teachers to use in classroom instruction.
- Summer Science Program, Halloween Happenings, holiday classes during school breaks.
- Adult education including lecture, field trips and educational travel.

**The Planetarium:**

- Planetarium shows Saturday and Sunday 2 p.m. and 3 p.m.
- Special shows as announced.
- Third largest facility of its type in the state.
- Changing multi-media shows.
- Special holiday programs.

**Memberships:**

| | |
|---|---:|
| Individual Membership | $25 |
| Family Membership | $40 |
| Contributing Members | $100 |
| Sponsoring Member | $250 |
| Corporate Membership | $500 |
| Corporate Benefactor | $1,000 |

**Statistics:**

| | |
|---|---:|
| Total annual attendance | 27,000 |
| Total annual school students | 8,846 |
| Planetarium annual attendance | 8,404 |
| Travel participants | 693 |
| Outreach program participation | 4,000 |

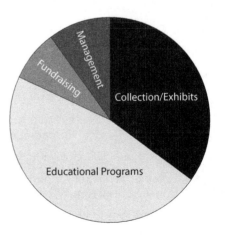

## Museum Income
Other
Bequests/Endowment
Admission Fees
Donations
Special Events
Educational Programs

## Museum Expenses
Management
Fundraising
Collection/Exhibits
Educational Programs

# Appendix H—10 Tips for Writing a Great Annual Report: Kick Annual Report Fear

From Kivi Leroux Miller

Even though nonprofit organizations aren't required to produce an annual report like publicly traded companies are, most nonprofit managers recognize the value of producing one. An annual report can help you demonstrate your accomplishments to current and future donors, cultivate new partnerships, and recognize important people.

But since an annual report isn't legally required, nonprofits often struggle with what should be included in an annual report and what should be left out. The following ten tips will help you craft an outstanding nonprofit annual report.

1. Focus on accomplishments, not activities in your annual report.

   We want to know what you did, but more importantly, we want to know why you did it. What were the results? Why did you spend your time and money the way you did? What difference did it make? Connect the everyday activities of your organization to your mission statement. Don't assume that readers will automatically understand how your activities help you achieve your mission. Connect the dots for them.

2. Jettison the administrative minutiae to get the most impact from your annual report.

   Getting a high-speed connection in the office and new accounting software might be big accomplishments from where you sit at your desk, but they have nothing to do with your mission. Inspire donors with accomplishments related to your mission in your annual report and leave all the administrative items for your board report.

3. Don't over-emphasize fundraising accomplishments in the annual report.

   Donors expect you to raise money, but fundraising accomplishments should not be celebrated in your annual report on the same level as your mission-related accomplishments. Readers are more interested in what you did with the money than how you raised it. While it is appropriate to include information on how well your fundraising efforts are going, it's best to place this information in the financial section of your report, rather than front and center.

4. Include photos in the annual report.

   Yes, photos really are worth a thousand words. Many of the people reading your annual report won't actually read it. Show them what you've been doing with photos. If you don't have a digital camera, get one now. It's also fine to use stock photography to illustrate your work. Type 'royalty free stock photos' in your favorite search engine and you'll find numerous sites.

5. Write captions that tell your story.

   Now that you've got them looking at the photos, tell a story with your captions. Don't just state what's in the photo. Connect the photo to an accomplishment. If people read nothing but the captions in your annual report, they should still get a sense for the good work you did last year.

6. Include personal profiles in the annual report.

   Donors will be more impressed with real stories about real people than general summaries of your work. Explain what you have accomplished overall, then humanize your statistics with some personal profiles. Highlight how your work helped a specific individual. Share a volunteer's story of how they made a positive difference.

7. Explain your financials.

   Many of your donors won't know how to read a financial statement or won't take the time to read it. Include a paragraph or two that explains in plain English what the tables say. Where does your money come from and how do you spend it? What are your main fundraising strategies? Did you implement any cost-savings measures this year?

8. If you need space, trim the donor lists in the annual report.

   Nonprofits need to strike a balance between using the space in their annual report to discuss their accomplishments and using it to recognize donors. If as much as half of your annual report is donor lists, you should consider scaling the lists back to make more room for text and photos. Smaller donors can be recognized in other ways, such as lists in newsletters.

9. Triple-check your donor lists.

   There's no better way to sabotage a future donation than to spell the donor's name wrong in your annual report. If you are uncertain about a name, don't guess. Check it with the donor. Also carefully check the names of government agencies and foundations that gave you grants. The names people call these organizations in conversation are often short-hand for the full legal names that belong in your annual report.

10. Tell donors how they can help.

Never leave a potential supporter hanging and wondering how they can help you. Once you've inspired them with the good works in your annual report, close by telling them how they can help you do more. How can they support you with their money or time? Do you offer planned giving options, for example? Will you accept gifts of stock? Can they use a credit card? Be clear about the best ways to help.

Reprinted with permission of Kivi Leroux Miller.

# Appendix I—Brainstorming Form

**Potential Business Donors for our Organization**

*Your Name:*_____

| Category | Name & Address | Potential Major Donor<br><br>Y or N | I will contact this person<br><br>Y or N |
|---|---|---|---|
| My accountant | | | |
| My car dealer | | | |
| My banker(s) | | | |
| My attorney | | | |
| Members of my professional association | | | |
| My insurance agent | | | |

| | | | |
|---|---|---|---|
| My doctor(s) | | | |
| | | | |
| My dentist(s) | | | |
| | | | |
| Members of a service club to which I belong | | | |
| | | | |
| | | | |
| | | | |
| Neighbors | | | |
| | | | |
| | | | |
| | | | |
| | | | |
| | | | |
| | | | |

| | | | |
|---|---|---|---|
| | | | |
| | | | |
| Relatives | | | |
| | | | |
| | | | |
| | | | |
| | | | |
| | | | |
| | | | |
| Clients/customers of mine | | | |
| | | | |
| | | | |
| | | | |
| | | | |
| | | | |

| | | | |
|---|---|---|---|
| Politicians I know | | | |
| | | | |
| | | | |
| | | | |
| | | | |
| | | | |
| | | | |
| | | | |
| People with whom I worship | | | |
| | | | |
| | | | |
| | | | |
| | | | |
| | | | |
| People with whom I work | | | |

| | | | |
|---|---|---|---|
| | | | |
| | | | |
| | | | |
| People with whom I went to school | | | |
| | | | |
| | | | |
| | | | |
| | | | |
| | | | |
| | | | |
| Parents of children with whom my children go to school | | | |
| | | | |
| | | | |
| | | | |
| | | | |

|  |  |  |  |
|---|---|---|---|
| My realtor |  |  |  |
|  |  |  |  |
| People with whom I do business |  |  |  |
|  |  |  |  |
|  |  |  |  |
|  |  |  |  |
|  |  |  |  |
|  |  |  |  |
|  |  |  |  |
| People with whom I play sports |  |  |  |
|  |  |  |  |
|  |  |  |  |
|  |  |  |  |
|  |  |  |  |

| | | | |
|---|---|---|---|
| | | | |
| | | | |
| People I know support other charities | | | |
| | | | |
| | | | |
| | | | |
| | | | |
| | | | |
| | | | |
| People who have asked me to support their favorite charity | | | |
| | | | |
| | | | |
| | | | |
| People I know who volunteer for other nonprofit organizations | | | |
| | | | |

|  |  |  |  |
|---|---|---|---|
|  |  |  |  |
|  |  |  |  |
|  |  |  |  |
| Others |  |  |  |
|  |  |  |  |
|  |  |  |  |
|  |  |  |  |
|  |  |  |  |
|  |  |  |  |

# Appendix J—Moves Management Corporate Intake Form

Contact Name_____

Title_____

Company Name_____

Address _____

Phone_____

Fax _____

E-mail_____

Website: _____

Type of Prospect:

☐ Sole Proprietorship ☐ Corporation
☐ LLC    ☐ Subchapter S Corp    ☐ Other or Unknown

☐ Volunteer Prospect:

☐ Board        ☐ Committee_____

☐ Solicitor_____

☐ Recruiter_____

☐ Ask Amount $_____

☐ Project/Program Requesting Funding_____

☐ History with our organization_____

☐ Referred by_____

☐ Areas of interest_____

Next Step:

☐ Assigned for cultivation to _____        Date_____

☐ Ask to serve on committee                          Date_____

☐ Invite to cultivation event                        Date_____

☐ Invited to cultivation event                       Date_____

☐ Attended cultivation event                         Date_____

☐ Agreed to serve on committee                Date_____

☐ Proposal/ask letter prepared                Date_____

☐ Ask for gift                                Date_____

☐ Solicited—pending response                  Date_____

☐ Declined                                    Date_____

☐ Solicit later                               Date_____

☐ Follow up information to be sent            Date_____

☐ Follow up information sent                  Date_____

☐ Acknowledgement letter sent                 Date_____

☐ Pledge reminder sent                        Date_____

☐ Recognition gift sent                       Date_____

☐ Future involvement suggested                Date_____

# Appendix K—NP Catalyst Corporate Giving Resource Guide

Dear Business Leader,

Your philanthropy is as unique and individual as your business. A giving plan can be a powerful tool. It can help your company personalize its giving and make sure community contributions are as strategic and meaningful as possible. By tailoring your giving plan to your company's mission, core strategies, personal and professional connections, and/or customer targets, you will maximize the opportunities associated with wise charitable decision-making. Whether formal or informal, these plans not only increase the satisfaction of your corporate philanthropy, they can also improve business-related and financial performance.

The NPCatalyst *Corporate Giving Resource Guide* is intended to help your business link values with community needs, establish goals and strategies for giving, involve key staff members, and evaluate the community-driven efforts with which you invest.

This resource guide was created to provide business leaders with ideas and tools to create and manage successful corporate giving plans.

*A tool for community leadership*

NPcatalyst's *Corporate Giving Resource Guide* is designed as a tool for successful corporate engagement. The resource guide:

◆ Briefly illustrates the steps involved in creating a rewarding and mutually-beneficial corporate giving program

◆ Serves as a resource when developing the giving program and philanthropic strategy

◆ Creates a connection to NPCatalyst, which seeks to advise, design, and/or manage optimal corporate giving programs

*Applying proper focus*

As an executive of a small or large business, you likely receive many requests for charitable support, either seeking volunteer leadership, in-kind or product contributions, or financial donations. Whichever the case (or all), it is quite possible that a formal giving process or strategy is not in place. As a result, charitable support from your business might represent more of a burden (or an after-thought) than an act of kindness or, for some, a cost of doing business. Without a strategy, your business will not derive the benefits it deserves from your giving.

The creation and management of effective giving programs should no longer be viewed upon as a negative or a burden.

A business's giving program is typically over and above its participation in local organizations, community foundations, or other workplace giving campaign initiatives. This resource guide will help you choose the options that are right for your business. It will take you through the basic steps of creating, organizing and improving your giving program that can help you take advantage of this potentially powerful business tool.

We have found that most businesses give to their communities because it is simply the right thing to do. Many business leaders have discovered that a well-thought out and designed giving program can help support their corporate mission and, at the same time, improve the company's bottom line.

*A business can do well by doing good.*

The bottom-line benefits of giving include:

❑ Enhanced reputation and standing in the community

❑ Greater customer loyalty.

❑ Competitive advantage in attracting and retaining employees.

❑ Increased positive name recognition and brand awareness.

❑ Closer relationships with community leaders and officials.

❑ Leadership development opportunities for employees.

❑ Beneficial business-to-business relationships with non-profits.

❑ A reservoir of goodwill within the community.

❑ Improved internal communications and sense of common purpose.

❑ Exposure of staff to new ideas, points of view, and important social movements.

❑ Increased revenue from clients you might not otherwise access.

❑ Healthier, more livable, and economically stronger communities.

If one or more of your business's goals are on this list, you're on the right path toward creating a successful corporate giving program.

*Align with business strategies*

If it's about increasing market share, hiring and retaining quality staff, creating strong B2B relationships, improving corporate culture, enhancing public image and, of course, providing outstanding community-beneficial resources and opportunities, then you're on the right path.

For some businesses, giving is based on the old model of "checkbook charity", signified by simply writing checks for causes and organizations. That model has since morphed into giving programs tailored to align charitable contributions (time, money, in-kind donations) with business goals, core strategies and desired benefits.

Business leaders representing forward-thinking, strategically-motivated charitable giving programs recognize clear connections between corporate health and the health of the communities in which they do business. They understand that corporate giving is not just a matter of conscience: it is also a matter of understanding the congruence of business and community goals.

*Determine the purpose of your giving plan*

It is important to address what you want your corporate contributions to accomplish. One way to do this is by determining where your company's interests intersect with those of the community. By designing a program to meet specific goals and objectives, you will have a program that is proactive instead of reactive--one that goes beyond simply responding to requests. Focused giving enables a company to make the greatest possible impact with its dollars. Questions to address when determining the purpose of your corporate giving plan are:

❑ What are your current business interests?

❑ What are your future business needs?

❑ What role does your company want to play in the community?

❑ What are your employees' interests and what causes are they committed to?

❑ What area of your community or who in the community is most affected by your business?

❑ What community issues are likely to affect your business and/or employees?

❑ What do you want your company to be known for?

❑ Whom are you trying to reach?

❑ What is the desired return on your charitable investment?

❑ How will measure success?

*Design the giving program*

The reasons that the vast majority of corporate giving programs are not successful are often because there are no purposes, responsibilities, and procedures. Furthermore, successful programs make sure to leverage giving to maximize optimal return on their charitable investment. Key steps and factors found in successful giving programs include:

❑ Hire a consultant, agent, or a point-of-contact employee.

❑ Create a mission statement for the corporate giving program.

❑ Establish a giving budget.

❑ Define the giving structure—direct contributions, company-sponsored foundation, or fund at a community foundation.

❑ Determine the preferred ways of giving—direct cash support, event sponsorships, restricted program contributions, in-kind or product donations.

❑ Establish written guidelines to communicate the program's goals and objectives.

❑ Develop policies and procedures as they relate to giving practices and decisions.

❑ Employing a clear strategy and process for tactfully saying "no."

❑ Create an advisory or charitable decisions committee to make funding recommendations.

❑ Create a decision-making process, featuring policies, procedures, and key responsibilities.

*The leadership element*

We've found that businesses believe that the passion and creativity of their employees emerge when they know their efforts make a difference. Knowing this, business leaders choose to create deeper engagement with community organizations, including those receiving their financial support. This is frequently represented through *employee volunteerism, pro-bono employee service or board leadership.* Some businesses have incorporated incentive and recognition programs for staff members who are active community supporters, including:

❑ Employee matching gift programs - match employee donations to charitable organizations;

❑ Employee Giving campaigns - focus on community awareness and fundraising;

❑ Employee volunteer support - cash grants to organizations where employees volunteer a certain amount of time;

❑ Employee volunteer time matching – compensating volunteer time at hourly rates or paid time off

❑ Business development incentives – driven from networking, new business relationships and revenue-generating channels.

*Leverage community engagement*

Very few people will recognize your corporation's community leadership if it's not properly leveraged. Whether it's taking advantage of the benefits offered through event sponsorships or naming opportunities through direct donations, it's incredibly important to monitor the deliverables, measure their effectiveness, and promote the achievements. Strategic and effective corporate-to-community engagement presents optimal opportunities to generate positive recognition, among many other benefits which are available through charitable support. To achieve this, we encourage business leaders to:

◆ Design a plan to monitor engagement and measure its effectiveness. This includes:

❑ Tracking volunteer hours and the impacted organizations

❑ Recording all financial contributions, the ways the money is gifted, and the desired usage of funds

❑ Evaluating the impact by determining if needs were met

❑ Capturing feedback from all giving stakeholders (decision committee, individual employee volunteers

◆ Craft a marketing plan to promote and communicate charitable activities

❑ Internally among employees, vendors, and customers

❑ Externally through traditional and social media

*Enlisting experts*

Businesses are encouraged to seek professional guidance and management. Among the services available from professionals are:

❑ Audit of gifting process

❑ Design of engagement/giving strategy

❏ Guide or facilitate contribution activities

❏ Deliver "insider" information and research

❏ Connect with nonprofit organizations. Enlisting the services of a professional often saves corporate time. Just like you hire experts to accomplish goals in technology and strategic planning, we recommend you hire experts to manage your corporate giving plan. By working with an expert you can save time executing the most effective and beneficial strategy.

Reprinted with permission of Peter Parker.

# Index

# FUNDRAI$ING
## as a Career

What, Are You Crazy?

www.charitychannel.com

# 50 A$KS
## in 50 Weeks

A Guide to Better Fundraising for
Your Small Development Shop

www.charitychannel.com

**PRESS**

# ASKING
## about Asking

### Mastering the Art of
### Conversational Fundraising™

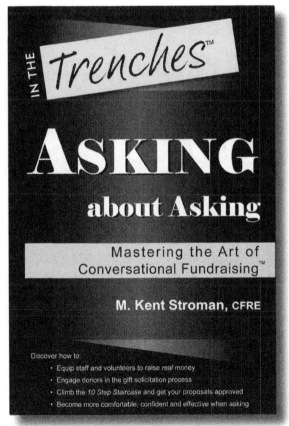

www.charitychannel.com

*Charity*Channel
**PRESS**™

# YOU AND YOUR Nonprofit

## Practical Advice and Tips from the CharityChannel Professional Community

www.charitychannel.com

# Capital
# Campaigns

## Everything You NEED to Know

IN THE

*Trenches*™

## Capital
## Campaigns

### Everything You NEED to Know

Linda Lysakowski, ACFRE

Discover how to:

- Conduct your capital campaign from start to finish
- Build a strong infrastructure for your campaign
- Develop a compelling campaign case statement
- Recruit volunteers for your campaign

www.charitychannel.com

*Charity*Channel
**PRESS**™

# Confessions
### of a Successful
# Grants Writer

## A Complete Guide to Discovering and Obtaining Funding

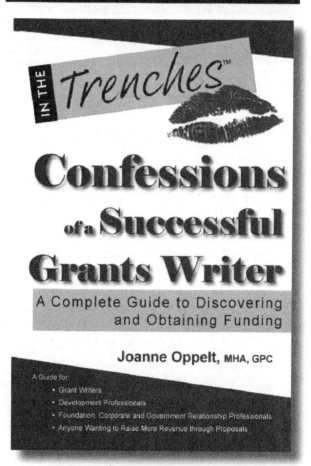

IN THE *Trenches*™

# Confessions
### of a Successful
# Grants Writer

## A Complete Guide to Discovering and Obtaining Funding

### Joanne Oppelt, MHA, GPC

A Guide for:

- Grant Writers
- Development Professionals
- Foundation, Corporate and Government Relationship Professionals
- Anyone Wanting to Raise More Revenue through Proposals

## www.charitychannel.com

*Charity*Channel
# PRESS

# Getting Started in
# Prospect Research

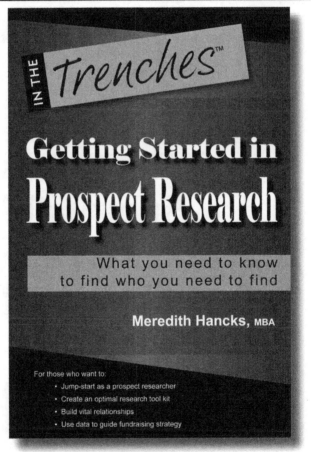

IN THE *Trenches*™

## Getting Started in
## Prospect Research

What you need to know
to find who you need to find

Meredith Hancks, MBA

For those who want to:
- Jump-start as a prospect researcher
- Create an optimal research tool kit
- Build vital relationships
- Use data to guide fundraising strategy

www.charitychannel.com

*Charity* Channel
**PRESS**™

CPSIA information can be obtained at www.ICGtesting.com
Printed in the USA
LVOW04s1402080115

422017LV00017B/196/P